Saboteur

By Burt Jay Rice

PAGE LEFT BLANK INTENTIONALLY

CONTENTS

PROLOGUE SHAKE-UP AT THE WHITE HOUSE

No one expected Vice President Damien Cromwell to ever become President. No one anticipated the President's plane—Air Force One— to plummet out of the sky during the second year of Andrew Clayburn's lackluster tenure.

Like most vice presidents, Cromwell's role had been as a policy "Yes Man." Officiator of events unworthy of President Andrew Clayburn's time, few knew of Cromwell's credentials. He had been recruited from the private sector over the objections of Clayburn's staff and advisors. Clayburn's rebuttal had been: "I know him. He's a good man . . . and who the hell cares about a V.P. anyway?" Consequently, when Cromwell took the reins from the go-along-to-get-along Clayburn, no one suspected his true leanings.

It wasn't long before the Cabinet found out. Three of them sat in the Oval Office casually, facing each other and aligned perpendicular to the president's desk. Cromwell, six-two, with wavy brown hair and slightly graying sideburns, sat at the head of the room and stared at them through unblinking brown eyes. "Gentlemen, I thank you for coming. I know most of you don't know me, so I'm happy to have this opportunity to meet you all."

The group included Secretary of State Charles Thebe, Treasury Secretary Morris Hines, and Attorney General, Arthur Gross. They accepted the tribute with obligatory nods. None of them harbored opinions about their new leader since they had hardly interacted with Cromwell except to exchange casual greetings in the Dirksen Senate Dining Room, or while occasionally passing his office in the Eisenhower Executive Building on the way to the White House. In their minds, he was merely the deceased President's shadow—an inconsequential attendee at cocktail parties with an exceptionally pretty wife.

To underscore Cromwell's lukewarm reception by the Washington elite, most of his cabinet had declined to attend the informal meeting, citing other obligations. The new president and the three present were aware that neither HUD nor Transportation had pressing matters on their agendas, though this observation remained unspoken.

Cromwell smiled. His deep-set eyes crinkled around the corners. "Well, I guess I'll forget about informal meetings, or next time, I'll be the only one here."

Uncomfortable laughter ensued.

"Wasn't that way when I called meetings at my company, Alternate Energy, back in Colorado. Guess I'll have to make my bones with you Washington guys." More uncomfortable laughter followed as his eyes drifted to the portraits of past presidents, as if seeking their assurance while he settled into his new job as the most powerful man in the free world.

"Sorta sorry that Energy Secretary Barnes isn't here. What I have to say might be of interest, but I'm sure at least one of you will pass it on."

Cromwell's sarcasm was not lost on the group. "As a clean energy guy, I have long been worrying about our backsliding in the extent and means of production of conventional sources, like oil, gas, shale, since the Republican gentleman left office a number of years ago."

The three attendees exchanged puzzled glances. They belonged to a party that had actively worked to reduce conventional energy production in response to the increasing support for clean energy among the younger generation. They wondered about the unexpected stance of this outsider.

The President, centered between the gold curtains and the two flags, reached for his glass of water. "I see from your faces that you expected Morris's approach to energy to continue." Cromwell shrugged. "Well, that would be wrong. We are again dependent upon the whims of the Saudis and their Emirate allies for a majority of our oil. The Russians are now in complete control of the European market and, with no sanctions for years, rogue states like Iran accumulate wealth daily to export terror."

Charles Thebe, who had been looking down at his shoes against the dark blue rug suddenly looked up, blurting out his resistance, "But Pres'dent Clayburn—"

"I know this comes as a surprise. Andy and I did not agree on everything but, believe me, he was coming to the same conclusion. Although he played politics well, he was a lover of our country above all. *As am I,* gentlemen." Cromwell's clear brown eyes calmly surveyed the group. "*As am I,* he repeated with emphasis. "You gentlemen don't know this, but I was about to resign from Alternate Energy, regardless."

Hines, a chubby man with wildly out of control hair, thrust forward violently. "But that was your baby, wasn't it.

Didn't you start the whole shift into solar and wind?"

"Yes, Mr. Hines—may I call you Morris?—that is definitely so. Your information was correct." The President was calm in the face of Hines's apparent agitation.

"I had a firsthand view as the industry developed and, believe me, it sickened me. Con artists flocked in by the carload. They pocketed money from sweetheart deals arranged by politicians drooling for campaign kickbacks, for projects that were a joke." He reflected for a moment. "It was like the gold rush all over again. No, gentlemen. We are not ready for alternatives at the expense of sane production. "

"But, Mr. President—"

"I didn't say we are giving up alternatives, Morris. Hopefully, with regulation, that industry may indeed be the future—but it certainly isn't there yet." He tilted forward in his high-backed chair with the Presidential Seal haloing his head. "And what about our foreign reserves? Not too long ago we were way ahead in the balance of payments. Our credit was the best." He studied Hines. "Our currency was the envy of the world, right Morris? You remember that don't you?"

Hines had to agree. "Uh . . . yes. That is so but—"

"Why a 'but'?"

"Well, our exports are cheaper this way."

Cromwell pursed his lips. "And what about our debt?"

Perspiration doused Hines's forehead. "Well, that's true, it's quite high, but some economists say—"

"And some economists say the other. I'm not going to be guided by people who have nothing at risk. America's prosperity is at stake. Am I clear?"

"Yessir," mumbled the chubby treasury secretary.

"Arthur." Cromwell shifted his focus to the AG. "You will start working on presidential orders to reduce restrictions on mining, drilling and the like. I expect them on my desk by early next week, so that we can fine-tune them."

Gross blew air through his thin lips, wriggling the thin mustache above. His plain face bore the pockmarks of early childhood maladies. His pale blond hair was too thin in many places to obscure the pinkness of his scalp. "As you wish, Mr. President. My staff will be on it this p.m.."

The president rose, inviting the others to do the same. The edges of his eyes crinkled. "I'm sure that this has been a surprise to you, gentlemen. Not quite what you expected, eh?" He strolled around in front of his desk and waited.

"Well, not exactly, suh." Charles Thebe, a thick man of six-feet with ramrod straight posture, drew the words out with his southern drawl. His notable college athleticism at Alabama was apparent in his movements, even after thirty some years. *"But, you ah the Pres'dent."*

Cromwell's smile remained but his eyes narrowed. "Yes, that's true, isn't it? Good afternoon, gentlemen."

***

The Harry S. Truman Office Building, home of the State Department, was like most D.C. government buildings: massive and sterile. The legions of tulips swarming the length of its front did nothing to soften its austere lines.

"Well, what the fuck do yuh genl'emen make of that?"

Thebe asked as Hines and Gross huddled on the huge couch in his own sizeable office. "How's that gonna play with them Saudis? We up to our ass in deals with 'em to screw the Russkies. Who we gonna use if they git pissed and pull out on us? Fucking Venezuela?"

"Hell no," said Gross. "Even if the communists were gone, their production won't be up to speed for years."

"And Iran and Iraq aren't going to help us—kill us, yes, help us, no." Thebe pulled a large cigar from his pocket. "Ana'one?"

Both men declined.

He bit off the tip and lit the other end with a heavy silver lighter. "So . . . where could this lead?"

"Oil shortages," said Gross. He straightened his mustache with a forefinger. "Lines at the pumps, hoarding . . ." he shook his head.

Hines ran his chubby fingers through his wild hair. "My God, what could they do to our investments? We have a deal with the Prince. All of us."

"Yeah, don' remind me." Thebe's cheeks creased inward as he took a massive puff. "Our understading with the Saudis will take a drastic turn and just fall flat. An' what's gonna happen with a lotta these bullshit windmills and solar batt'ry op'rations when they really gotta produce? What a fuckin' fiasca tha's gonna be."

"And my investments, uhh." Hines's hands dropped to his lap like wounded pigeons.

Gross sniffed. "I guess you should have stayed at Harvard, Hines. The real world is much too dangerous, isn't it?"

Thebe thrust his cigar at Gross. "Hey, ah ain't too happy neither, Arthuh. Ah got a mess invested in that alternative energy shit, too. Won' mean a thaing if it ain't got real oil to make up for the inevitable shortfall. Yuh kin make money on solar as a backup, but not when it has ta carry the whole fuckin' load. Ain't worth a shit as an inve'sment then. An' there's ma family, an' business fren's and people I'm countin' on aftuh ah resign in a coupla years. They all gon'na hate mah guts."

Thebe watched the delicate trail of smoke weave upward. "An' how 'bout those nutty clean energy freaks? Whatta they gonna do when th' drillin' starts up—sheet. Yuh gonna have all those millennials as well as aging hippies and environmental terrorists outta sorts." He shook his cigar at the ceiling. "Pres'dent Anduh Clayburn, whah the fuck did yuh decide ta git in that fuckin' plane? Yuh didn' have nowhere special ta go. Jus' an' ol' speech ta some ancient vetr'ans." He shook his cigar at the ceiling. "Lookit the trouble yuh causin'. If yuh was here ah'd smack ya, bless yuh soul." The Secretary of State smiled at his close friend's memory. "Well, gen'nelmen, if yuh done with yuh 'spensive cognac ah guess ya'all betta' scoot. We got ou'selves a shit storm ta deal with."

CHAPTER 1 THE ENERGY ISSUE

Light from the dazzling chandelier in the center of the great hall at the Al-Yamama Palace in Riyadh illuminated the concave bowl at the ceiling's center. It overflowed to the concentric circles around the bowl and reflected against the Italian marble floor beneath.

Under the great circle of light, two Saudi Princes spoke in low tones. Although they were the only inhabitants of the great hall, the arrest of three of their cousins some years before had rendered them even more cautious than ever. The massive palace was known to have "ears."

As was the wont of the younger princes, Mohammed Bin Salman and his younger brother, Sultan, wore business suits. Sultan, always the more emotional, was irate. His face flushed as he threw his hands into the air. "This new American President will betray us. My friends in the American Embassy say the rumors and speculation are all over Washington. If America goes back to shale production, we could be ruined."

"Peace, Brother," Mohammed extended a palm toward the other's shoulder, reminding him that their voices carried in this location. As Sultan calmed, Mohammed reassured him. "I also have sources and they tell me that he will be smashed by the liberal press and his own party. They are committed to ridiculous 'green' energy and they control both their House and Senate. As the Americans say, 'he doesn't stand a chance'."

"Still," Sultan relinquished ground to his brother, as he

had always done since they were children, "I say that we must start calling in the loans we have made to their politicians unless they stop him. How many shares in Aramco do those thieves own, thanks to our King's generosity—"

"And the even more generous nature of our cousin Suliman, who, as we know, is now the power behind the throne."

"Yes, Brother," Sultan agreed, "our royal prince has promoted our interests admirably since he relieved the others of their responsibilities."

"What a quaint description, Sultan," laughed Mohammed. "You always paint a rosy picture of everything. They were arrested."

"Yes, yes, my dear brother," Sultan nodded, laughing at his own foible. "You are right. *You are right,*" he added again. "Anyway, I believe many of the Americans' Cabinet and party leaders also owe us much."

"Just like Ukraine. These Americans are such liars. At least we admit to bribery and corruption as a necessary way of life, but they—"

"I know, Mohammed, they are incredible hypocrites." Sultan shook his head, laughing. "They lie even to themselves . . . so pure . . . so honest—"

"'So full of shit,' as the Americans say."

Their laughter rose toward the lighted dome above and echoed along the walls of the great hall.

***

The Kremlin office felt powerful and full of history. Tall bookcases made of dark wood reached almost to the high ceilings. This building was built in 1787 by Catherine the Great, and over the years, it had seen Russia go from monarchy to totalitarianism, to a brief, flash-in-the-pan democracy and, in the opinion of many, back to totalitarianism again.

Sunlight from tall draped windows illuminated dancing motes as they lit the desk of Yuri Karmov. The Russian President had been unanimously re-elected for a term of sixteen years, of which ten remained. The office was business-like, with few frills or extraneous decorations except for two massive chandeliers of historic origin. A number of high-backed chairs surrounded the extension protruding from his desk. Seated were Nikolai Patrovich, Secretary of the Security Council, Prime Minister Dmitry Medroskev, and Igor Sechinov, chief executive of the state oil company, Rosneft. All faced a young man who stood before them.

Karmov's cold blue eyes focused upon the nervous young man. "Please review what you have told me about the direction of this new president, Damien Cromwell, Yuri Vladnikov."

Vladnikov was of medium height with pallid skin and a nervous tick in his left eye. His voice was so thin that the others had to lean forward to hear him. Karmov did not. He had already grilled the young man intensively before presenting him to his advisors.

"Our research tells us that the new president intends to revitalize the defunct shale oil industry," the young man said.

Yes, research, thought Patrovich, covering his

amusement with a cough. *About ten percent research and ninety percent espionage, if you were honest, young man. We are a nation of euphemisms.*

"It is our expectation," Vladnikov continued, "that he will infuse substantial capital into the industry. As you know, it was first devastated by the coronavirus outbreak, when utilization dropped drastically. That, coupled with the surplus in oil due to our 'unfortunate disagreement' with the Saudis, led to prices that dropped below thirty dollars a barrel, before American policy changed back in early 2020. Many of the fracking companies had borrowed heavily for equipment, unlike the established oil companies—"

"Yes, yes." Sechinov threw up a slim hand. A dazzling stone which rode his third finger, splashed light across his face as he gestured. "We know this history. Most of them failed or were about to until Trump bailed them out after the outbreak was over. During his second term they thrived, dropping our revenues precipitously. Only when Clayburn's constituents demanded sweeping restrictions on their oil production and he removed the sanctions on our pipeline to Europe—only then did we recover our rightful share of the market."

Prime Minister Dimity Medroskev, a bear of a man, *cracked* a pencil between his powerful hands. "Pah. And this wolf in sheep's clothing . . . this Cromwell bastard is going to aid those fucking frackers again?"

Vladnikov recoiled from the Prime Minister's rant. He stepped back and, with a deep breath, went on, "Yes. Our researchers tell us that he will create tax credits and loan availability in the industry. Already we see signs of vastly increased activity."

Sechinov fumbled with a pack of cigarettes, then stuffed it back into his pocket. Karmov, a health fanatic, did not approve of smoking.

Vladnikov said, "Between this and the Saudis, we will lose much of the European market. They have not been happy with our price increases over the last few years." He opened his hands, palms up. "But we had to raise them with all the losses before their Democrats came back to office. And then with Ukraine—"

"Let's not rehash old news," interjected Karmov. He stared up at the ceiling. "Is it not better to have the stability that we have with our consistent government?" He smiled.

All agreed vehemently.

"Well," said Karmov, "we shall have to see." He formed a steeple with his fingers. "We certainly will. Thank you all and you, especially, Yuri Vladnikov." The meeting was clearly over.

***

With all its modern buildings set before a backdrop of mountains sprinkled with snow, Tehran could be taken for Salt Lake City from afar. Sitting in one of the few forested areas of the densely populated city is the House of Leadership. Near the great assembly hall, where he addresses massive assemblies from a large podium, is the office of the Supreme Leader.

Since the death of Ali Khamenei, a younger and more progressive Akbar had effectively navigated international tensions with far more aplomb. Embargos had lifted and oil flowed regularly to its primary customer, China. To the displeasure of the hardliners and delight of the nation's youth, religion's role gradually receded and prosperity was taking hold. Prospects were positive—until a week ago. Now, in Rouhani's modest office, gloom engulfed the attendees. A new American president had been sworn in and Iran's ally Russia expressed concern.

Ali Katasi, Minister of Energy, was dressed in western apparel made popular by Rouhani. He sighed inwardly, thinking, *Oil, oil, it is always about oil in the long run. Our only lifeblood except for a bit of tourism. I hate the stuff. With our ability, we could compete in industry and science, but the oil addiction of the old times has held us back.*

He turned his attention to Rouhani's words. "My dear gentlemen, it looks as if the United States is again on a path of energy independence." The Supreme Leader shook his lightly bearded head. "The Russians are positively distraught but, with Europe, they have more reliable markets than do we. Japan and India have no love for us. If American shale oil were again available, they would gladly switch, as would South Korea. The Chinese, our biggest market, are loyal for now, but who can trust them if less expensive oil is available in quantity?"

"Just as we have been getting back on our feet," rasped Foreign Minister Ebrahim Zariff. "The Devils are at our throats again." At that, all attendees emitted similar pronouncements. The Great Satan and its accomplice, Israel, were damned before Allah for many minutes.

Finally, Rouhani raised his hands. "My friends, Allah will do his share I am sure, but must we not do ours?"

"And what precisely is ours?" blurted the youthful

Mansour Katasi.

The elders frowned but Rouhani merely smiled.

"That, my young Minister of Youth Affairs, remains to be seen."

CHAPTER 2 BEIRUT

The southern quarter of Beirut is known as Al Dahya. Even its newer high-rises, funded by Iran after the July war of 2006, are a bit more squalid than in other locations. Gangs prowl its streets by night. Fittingly, it is also the home of Hezbollah's central headquarters and that of thousands of its fighters. Since the civil war, Hezbollah is the only paramilitary group allowed to maintain its weapons. Additional arms are supplied by Iran and Syria. Not so coincidentally, it also wields significant power, including a number of seats in Parliament.

The tall man's European style clothes were in stark contrast to the khaki and greens of the men passing on the narrow sidewalk. He wore no beard. His eyes were blue as blue could be and his figure was erect and solid. The bulge beneath his tailored jacket was unmistakable.

Swarthy Hezbollah fighters eyed him with barely suppressed hostility. But, remarkably, he was allowed to pass without confrontation despite the unflattering comments in his wake. Since the stranger was fluent in both Arabic and Farsi, their vile references did not go unnoticed. With effort, he fought the tempting impulse to crush a few windpipes.

Huge posters plastered the walls honoring the Supreme Leader and Hezbollah. Black, green, yellow and red flags hung listlessly in the stifling air. All symbolized Muslim beliefs that he once knew but couldn't quite remember any more.

The man noticed spray paint covering women's anatomies on billboards. *Bikinis* not *going to make sales here,* he thought. Even ads for cosmetics were similarly vandalized. *As I remember, these were the most boring characters I ever worked with, but the money was good,* he thought.

Ahead was the Security Corner or Almurab'a Alamni, Hezbollah's headquarters. Cameras populated the streets and alleys and protruded from buildings, like a hundred eyes. In the twilight, shadowy figures flowed to and fro, stopping anyone who didn't have the day's code.

A bearded man in khaki with a military-style button-down shirt and a carefully trimmed beard halted his progress. The tall man responded to the curt question and was beckoned toward the door of a squat two-story building. Hazy shadows in the courtyard monitored his progress.

Once inside, another silent man, this one in green, led him down a long hall. From an open doorway he heard the afternoon prayer. His escort knocked at a solid door of dark wood. As it opened, the second man melted back into the dimness of the scantily lit corridor. The glare from harsh and focused spotlights blinded him.

"There is a chair in front of you. Please sit," a voice spoke from within the room.

"What is—"

"I will ask the questions, if you do not mind." The voice was calm but with a touch of steel that brooked no disagreement. "You are Phillip Sydney?"

"For our purposes."

The calm in the voice became strained. "What does that mean?"

"It will do for our purposes."

"Oh, so you are a man of mystery?"

"One has to be to stay alive. Now, could we get to business?"

The man's voice heightened a full octave. It was obvious that he was used to respect. "Yes. Yes, we shall." There was a pause and the sound of liquid pouring. "Would you care for water?"

"No, thank you. I'm perfectly fine."

Behind the impenetrable wall of light, liquid splashed into a glass. "Are you
aware of your mission?"

"Of course."

" And you know how deadly the ampules we give you can be?"

"Naturally."

"And your price?"

"Fine. Half was already transmitted to my account in Switzerland, and the dollar is strong."

"Yes. And the rest upon completion, also in U.S. dollars?"

"Just as agreed," said the tall man. He started to rise.

"One more thing . . . there is a condition. You will take two of my best people with you."

"That wasn't what I understood. I made it clear that I work alone."

Irritation in the voice behind the harsh lights was palpable. "This is *my* operation. It will be on *my* head if anything goes wrong and that is something that *I* am not willing to concede to your 'lone wolf' preference. It is *non-negotiable, Mr. Phillip Sydney!"*

No arguing with this one. His Arab ego is on the line. Sydney exhaled air through his lips. *If his rules become unsustainable, my companions can always be eliminated.* "All right," he conceded, "Done."

"Excellent. You will be our guest tonight and introductions will be made tomorrow. Good night to you, Mr. Sydney. The man outside will show you your room and arrange for food."

***

Sydney was awakened early by morning prayers. They reverberated through the corridor and, he supposed, through mosques and residences throughout the quarter. *It's tedious,* he thought. *I don't know what Obama thought was so scintillating about the whole thing.* Sydney frowned. *Didn't he say it was the most beautiful of sounds? Well, who am I to argue with an American President?*

In a small room, sparsely furnished with a plain table and four chairs, he met his team. A tall man with thick shoulders in green fatigues and a woman with the largest dark eyes he had ever seen. She, too, wore fatigues of the same color. They were busily eating fried eggs and thick toast.

Sydney nodded. *Eggs are hallal,* he thought, referring to his vast repertoire of facts from operations the world over. *Suits me.* A small man in a modified turban appeared. *He has clerical connections,* surmised Sydney. When he ordered similar fare in Farsi, both of his companions looked up.

"So you speak the Iranian tongue?" asked the man. His voice rumbled from deep in his barrel chest.

Not to start off on the wrong foot, Sydney smiled and said, "Yes, it has been my good fortune to learn the language, although I am sure my pronunciation is poor."

"Look, my friend," the man switched to accented but precise English, "if we are to get along, let's be honest with each other. You speak excellent Farsi and I speak good English, so let us stop with all the flowery B.S. My name is Kassim Al-Musawi."

Sydney eyed the man, taking his measure. *Not bound by Mohammed's rule on objectionable language. Good. That makes life easier.* "Okay, Kassim Al-Musawi, as you wish. No bullshit."

The woman fingered her niqab. "I am Dalia. This will be gone once we are clear of these chauvinists. I hate it." Despite her displeasure, her tone was soothing as a soft breeze.

Betraying his usually unflappable nature, Sydney's light eyebrows rose deep into his smooth forehead.

"I studied at your Berkely," she explained. "Sometimes it gets me in trouble but I'm a good fighter, so they put up with me."

Sydney sipped his water. Sharia law in the sector forbade much else. "What do you know of our mission?"

"Nothing, except it is to punish the Americans," said Al-Musawi. "That is a

blessing. I hate America."

"And you, Dalia?" He turned to look at the only part of

herself he could see. Her eyes narrowed above the veil.

"Look at how we have to live. Fugitives in our own country, scorned and ridiculed by America who loves Israel and hates us. *Israel*—who took our land and persecutes our brothers, the Palestinians, who have no homeland because of them. We understood in Berkley, but the rest of America didn't. The rich, complacent Americans must pay for the pain they cause."

Sydney studied her raging eyes. *Not exactly the case, my dear. The Palestinians were a bunch of thugs and kicked out of every country which accepted them—but, for my purposes, your hatred works. Although she sounds a little canned and a bit unconvincing, I wonder how deep it really goes. We shall see.* He lifted a paper napkin to his mouth. It was large and of good quality. He laughed inwardly. *The leaders always seem to have the best supplies, best food and best living accommodations. It's always the same no matter where. They live well and the troops suffer. They're all a bunch of phonies. And the game goes on.*

"All right. Do you both remember the coronavirus epidemic of two thousand twenty?"

Al-Musawi snorted. "Of course. I was in Tehran. Thousands died."

"Well, we are going to hit the United States harder than that," Sydney said.

Both of his companions frowned.

Sydney's full lips parted, exposing a row of perfect teeth. "Forgive the hyperbole. We are going to damage America's economy. That hurts them the worst. Sound good?"

"Yes." Dalia hesitated. Then quickly said, "Very, very good."

Al-Musawi merely nodded, stroking his well-trimmed beard with thick fingers.

Sydney fingered the top button of his jacket, releasing it, then the next. "Too hot for this. I won't be needing it for a while, anyway." He removed the jacket, tossing it carelessly to the floor to shock them. Next, his eyes radiated a frightening energy as he spoke very slowly. "Are you both sure? Be *very* sure, now. Later will be too late. Many, many may die, although that is not the intent." His gaze fell on Dalia. "If you hesitate or panic . . . I will kill you."

Both stared at the man. They had seen many frightening things in their careers of mayhem but the cold depth of those eyes was like drowning in an endless frigid ocean. Startled, Al-Musawi and the girl took a moment before responding.

I have just seen the devil, thought Dalia. Yet she couldn't explain the thrill that accompanied her fear.

"Well?" Sydney inquired. His voice like a dagger probing them. "It's no disgrace if you decide to leave now. After will be much too late."

The big Muslim regained his composure first. "I have killed many in the name of my God. I will never flinch from what is His will."

With a deep breath, Dalia said, "I will savor my revenge each moment."

The fire in Sydney's eyes dissipated. Once again his

tone was pleasant and reasonable. "Good. Now I have to excuse myself. There are some plans to be made." He checked his expensive smart watch. "It's now nine-ten. We should leave by eleven." He rose with a polite nod and walked purposefully out the door.

***

Karmov replaced the phone on his desk. Flexing his forearms in the habitual isometrics while at his desk, he thought, *the Iranians are impossible. Too many of these* fanatics *are already here in my country. If they overpopulate here like the rabbits they are, we will have to exterminate them. Still, for now they are useful. Their mercenary is in Beirut and ready to move. His price is high, but the cost will be shared by the Ayatollahs and the Saudis. I only hope the fools picked someone good, but I couldn't get involved. If this fails,* he smiled, *I want, as the Americans say, "plausible deniability."*

The Russian President compressed his hands and pushed until his face reddened. *Now we shall wait and see.*

***

According to the bearded Hezbollah soldier who drove them to Beirut-Rafic Hariri Airport, Tuesdays in the late afternoon were the least crowded. His dark eyes darted in all directions before he handed Sydney a small but dense platic box. There were no warnings on its shiny surface but Sydney placed it gingerly into a false compartment inside his toilet case. The spot was the safest bet to go unnoticed if someone checked through his small suitcase. Lastly, he was handed tickets to Mexico City and wished Allah's blessings.

A transparent ceiling above the terminal revealed sunlit clouds between its crisscrossing girders. The Alitalia non-stop was on schedule. There was no sightseeing. Sydney's hosts had dropped the team off without time to spare.

Don't want us to see the forbidden luxuries of decadent religions outside of their drab quarter, Sydney smiled. *Too bad, my Muslim friends. I surround myself with as many of those decadent delights as my pocketbook will allow—which, after this, should be unlimited.*

Whistling a tune of his own creation, the tall man made his way to the gate.

CHAPTER 3 "A MAN OF MYSTERY"

They rented a car at Benito Juarez International Airport under one of Sydney's false credit cards and international driver's licenses, before seeking lodging nearby.

Early the next morning, they drove down Paseo de la Reforma to the Iranian Embassy. Its huge red, white and green flags flanked the modern building which stood amidst a number of elegant structures housing other embassies, each with its individual garden of gardenias and bougainvillea.

Dalia had discarded her niqab early into their flight. She now wore a blonde wig with red lip color spread lavishly on her mouth. Something that no Muslim woman would possibly wear. Only she entered the classic building with tall arched windows. Below the great patio in front, Mexico City's skyline gleamed behind the embassy's trees.

Upon giving her fictitious name, Dalia was quickly escorted into a small room. A large picture of the Ayatollah dominated, with smaller pictures of current leaders beneath. Dalia was appalled at the opulence of the building. *How many more weapons would those tapestries and vases buy,* she wondered. *How much food for starving Palestinian children could those fine pictures, elegant chairs, gilt-edged tables and brocaded couches provide?*

A large man with a toothy smile rose from his desk. He nodded but failed to make physical contact or introduce himself. Then he sat back and lifted a courier sack from the floor. "Please sit. I am instructed to provide you with a number of items. Let us make sure we have everything. Here is cash in pesos and dollars." He slid over bound stacks of currency. Next, he displayed an abundant array of passports and driver's licenses. "I hope these pictures do you justice."

He waited for her response to his attempted humor. When she merely smiled, he continued a bit more sharply. "Here are some special papers such as birth certificates and other detailed documents from a number of countries, but I doubt that you will need so much detail." The man smiled again although his eyes went to his expensive watch. "Your handbag is adequate?"

"Yes, thank you." Dalia swept the contents on the desk into a large leather purse.

He rose. "Well, if that is all, I must meet some other visitors. You should be aware that footage of this visit will be removed from our security cameras and that we will disclaim any knowledge of this meeting. We cannot afford to jeopardize our relations with Mexico." Without awaiting her response, the man motioned Dalia to the door. Neither said goodbye. Dalia walked slowly toward the parked car under the trees.

***

The trip to Nuevo Laredo was twelve hours and Sydney was anxious to start. When a mission was underway, his adrenalin drove him to complete it. Once outside of Mexico City, traffic along Route 57 was sparse. The group had had little to say during the many hours. On the flight, it was understandable, but Sydney reasoned that communication, and even some form of friendship, was necessary for a cohesive team. *Hell, I've crewed with outright enemies and made it work, so this shouldn't be that hard even if they're Muslims and not my preference for social companions.*

He did his best to make conversation. "We don't want to come into Texas at border crossings. That's why Nuevo Laredo."

In response, they merely nodded.

All right, he thought, *got to try harder.* With little traffic noise, it was easy to be heard in the smooth running vehicle. "In case you're wondering, I know of contacts that will get us into the United States, undetected. They are known as 'Coyotes,' and they specialize in routes that are unpatrolled."

Dalia turned toward him.

She is quite lovely as a blonde, thought Sydney. *Ah, women . . . even if they are dedicated killers. Why I remember that Swedish witch who fucked me to death, then tried to shove a fork through my eye—enough . . . concentrate Keen--uh . . . yes, it's 'Phillip.' That's who I am for this project. I've got to remember not to slip again, even in my mind.*

"What about the famous border wall? We heard it was impossible to climb," Dalia said.

Sydney shrugged. "I suppose, but to the east, where we will be, there are still areas that weren't completed."

"Because the Americans can't agree on anything," spat out Al-Musawi. "Not even to preserve their country. The fools don't deserve what they have and with the help of Allah, soon it may all be gone. Then those pampered weaklings will know what it is to live a life of wanting!"

Sydney was pleased. *Looks like we're talking. That's a start.* "Texas has plenty of border openings. That's where we'll get in." He drew a pack of English Hetfields from his pocket, offering it to the others.

Both vigorously declined.

Sydney laughed. "Well, I suspect I'll die from something far more immediate than these before I'm done." He expertly flipped one between his lips. Snapping open a Zippo Windproof, he lit up. "Anyhow, these men know the ropes . . ." he sought out Al-Musawi in the rearview.

"I am acquainted with the idiom," the big man responded. "I, too, am proficient in English, my friend."

"Okay," said Sydney. "Didn't mean to offend. Anyway, they are experts at penetrating." His lips compressed. "But, one thing to remember, both of you. These are cartel men. Cartels have little honor, so stay alert." Smiling once again he said, "They will provide our weapons, as well. I expect they will have a wide assortment, so choose your favorites. It'll be like Christ—like a holiday," he corrected, "so feel free."

This man is complex, thought Dalia. *Sophisticated, yet those eyes can freeze you as if you were in the coldest place in eternity.* "Sydney, where are you from?" she dared to ask.

He took a long puff, pouring it out through pursed lips. "Well, that's a complicated question. You might say South Africa, but there have been so many places since, I can't really say."

Dalia studied his profile: Roman nose, high cheekbones, deep tan. *Or you don't want to,* she thought.

He does have an accent but I can't quite place it.

He no longer wore the suit in which she had met him. Now, his arms, extended upon the wheel, were bared by his casual sport shirt. She noticed the jagged veins along his biceps, continuing into thick forearms. *He looked slim under that suit,* she thought, *but this is a* man, a man who cares about his bodily strength. Despite herself, her groin tingled. A sure sign of attraction.

Hell, I don't give a damn about the religion, anyway. I decided it was all bullshit at college—women in veils walking meekly behind their chauvinist husbands, beaten for even looking at another man—what bullshit! Any man who treated me that way would find a hot poker up his ass. She continued to study Sydney again out of the corner of her eye. He was preoccupied with the road. *Maybe we shall see what happens, my Mystery Man.*

***

When they arrived, Nuevo Laredo was dark. Sydney's GPS guided them through back roads and lighted houses. "Sorry we won't see the downtown nightlife," he quipped, "but we are going straight to the place they told us."

They drove under a railroad trestle into a street that seemed to have nothing but shadowy trees on one side and tall metal fences with gates on the other. As they stopped before one, the gate slid open. Inside was an old wooden house. It was rather small and in disrepair. Lights shone through the cracks in skewed window blinds. A slim moon revealed room to park on gravel patches interspersed between sand and scrubby grass. Beyond the dwelling, shadowy trees twisted and swayed. "I believe that breeze is coming off the Rio Grande," volunteered Sydney.

A door swung open. The outline of a large man was clear. He waved his arms, casting shadows that crept nearly to their feet. "Welcome, Senores." When Dalia approached he said, "Ah, Senorita, entre, come een." He nodded to someone past them. A small man *crunched* gravel as he approached. "Geef Juan your keys. He weell bring een your luggage."

The interior was surprisingly modern, if not lavish. Couches and chairs looked straight out of budget furniture ads. A full bar of reflective glass stood to their right. One of the largest televisions that Sydney had ever seen reflected soccer players and referees chasing around a field.

"You weel be our guests unteel tomorrow night. I hope you weel be comfortable. My name is Gilberto. I am here to make sure you are happy as my employers' honor-ed guests. Eef you need anything, you weel please tell me."

Sydney stepped toward the bar. "Well, Gilberto, what is the plan?" He reached for a Bowmore scotch, pouring it neat into a glass. He sipped. "Um. Your employers have excellent taste."

Gilberto had a large, moon face, indented with pock scars. His smile reflected many gold teeth. "I ahm hoppy, Senor Seedney. Very hoppy." Gilberto squinted. "Ah, the plan. Yes. We have thees house because eet is close to the river." He pointed to the right. "Not more than a soccer field or two away. That means very close,' he explained. "Although we are not far from El Centro—the center of Nuevo Laredo—here ees a leetle isolated. Old houses and muchos trees. No one cares much about thees neighborhood." He pointed to the floor. "On the other side of river," he pointed to the right again, "lots of sand and rocks and brush weeth only scattered trailers y casas, called Ranchos Penitas. We are very successful aiding access to the United States from here."

Aiding access. Quaint, thought Sydney. "Who is 'we'," he asked, although he already knew.

Gilberto positively glowed. "Why, our cartel in Nuevo Laredo. We are soon thee beegest, I theenk."

"Can we trust you?" said Musawi.

Sydney cringed inwardly. *I told him to let me do the talking.*

Gilberto's smile disappeared like sunlight behind a cloud. He tugged his slouching body upright. "Senor, we are men of honor."

Sydney threw up his hands. "I'm sure. I'm sure. Please forgive my friend's bluntness. It has been a long trip."

There was a nervous moment. Then Gilberto's huge smile was back. "Of course. Si' como no? A long treep."

The meal was tacos and frijoles. Al-Musawi declined the meat-filled variety but seemed to enjoy the rest. After dinner, Dalia yawned mightily.

Gilberto rose, eyeing the remainder of his third helping longingly. "You are tired, my frens. I will show you to your rooms."

"And then finish your dinner," laughed Sydney.

Gilberto frowned, then recognized his guest's quip. His face nearly split from a huge smile. "Ah, sí. Sí. Ha, ha, sí. Then I feenish. Ha, ha."

CHAPTER 4 MEETING THE CARTEL

The three slept late into the day. Separate rooms for each of them had been made comfortable with foam mattresses and soft sheets. When they entered the living room, the table was filled with decanters of coffee, stacks of tortillas and butter. Gilberto came out from the kitchen, his huge face beaming. Around his heavy middle hung an apron declaring in English, *Don't mess with the chef.* "We cahn have juevos and frutas. Whatever you wan.'"

After cleaning up, Gilberto pointed to a glowing window. "Eet ees una dia magnifica. You haf teel four thirty before the boss comes. He weel explain eferytheeng." He shrugged. "Eet ess boring here but there ees a park across the street. Jus' don' get lost."

Sydney squinted into the sharp sunlight. The "park" named, "Garden de los Ninos Revolucion," according to Gilberto, was no more than some low buildings and a sandy field with trails of scrub brush crisscrossing its perimeter. "So much for sightseeing," he remarked.

Dalia sighed. She had dispensed with her wig. Gilberto's heavy eyebrows rose at her transition, but he didn't comment. "Let's, at least, walk. I need some air, even if it is roasting hot," she said.

"I will go back to bed," Al-Musawi said.

"A man of few words," said Sydney, after their companion left.

"But a great fighter, according to my brothers," Dalia replied, as the two of them emerged into the street.

On the right were high fences and gates, painted and in remarkably good repair regardless of the ramshackle nature of the dwellings they protected. The air was heavy and thick. Five small boys kicked a nearly flat soccer ball along the dusty road. Their severely smudged clothes and grimy faces indicated a long match. Occasionally, an aging model car or truck forced them to the side, evoking a high-pitched chorus of "Puta! Puta!" when the

driver was safely beyond hearing distance. Dalia wiped her brow with the back of her hand, slightly smudging her forehead. "Where do they get the energy?"

"Kids," Sydney said.

"I wanted to play football when I was little," Dalia mused. "But the neighborhood I come from wasn't a place for little girls to indulge in a sport that has 'only for boys' stamped on it." Sydney said nothing. "Sorry," she said, "do you call it soccer? Oh, I remember you are not from America."

"I've never been a fan of the game," he said, looking past the clamoring kids. He became aware of her gaze and looked at her. "Football," he said with a brief nod.

After thirty minutes of soaking heat, they gave up and returned to the house.

"You do not care for our summer?" Gilberto snorted a laugh as he watched them drag in and flop down on whatever was close.

Dalia swiped at her drooping hair. She lifted it up, exposing her lovely neck, before bunching it behind her head. "I have been in deserts that were cooler."

Sydney smiled at the exaggeration, but said nothing.

The heat seemed to hang in the air like the incessantly buzzing insects.

"Why don' you shower? Lunch weel be on thee table." Gilberto spread his thick hands. "You do what you wan' teel four thirty. Then you meet thee boss."

***

As opposed to the grinning Gilberto, the small man facing them at the table had sharp eyes and a face that could watch you die without batting an eye. The thin lips below a narrow black mustache struggled to smile, letting through flashes of tobacco-stained teeth.

"Senores and Senorita, my name is Eduardo Flores." He casually flipped his hand toward a monster of a man behind him. "This is my associate. Just call him Luta. We are going to go over the plan now. Would anyone like coffee. No?" He paused, seeming to savor a moment of silence. " Very well. As you know, the Rio Grande' is a few hundred yards away. We have a raft—very safe this time of year— and on the other side, a van to take you to our secure house."

Sydney began, "We seem to be right in the middle of the Laredos—"

Light glinted from the large stone on his middle finger as Flores gestured with a raised hand. "Do not worry, Senor Sydney. Although we are close to both cities, there is little or no danger of our being caught. We have done this many times. The river's shores are quite deserted as is Ranchos Penitas, where we will conclude our business on the other side." His smile slipped. "We are a very large and powerful organization. We do not take chances. When I say 'deserted,' it is for sure." His insincere smile returned. "Comprende, Senor?"

"Si, comprendo," said Sydney.

Flores sipped the coffee. "And now to business." He replaced the cup, decorated by a grouchy rabbit that proclaimed "Don't ask me what's up before my coffee?" which Sydney translated silently from the Spanish.

"Our contract is for three hundred thousand dollars, am I correct?" Flores asked upfront.

"For the three of us?" Sydney answered.

"Si, Senor. For the three."

"Half now and half later," Sydney added.

Flores frowned. "I am not used to bargaining but my associates agreed, so . . . " his mustache barely moved as his tight lips rose, " . . . as you wish, Senor."

"Gracias. It is as I wish."

Flores's nod did not hide the anger radiated by his piercing eyes.

Sydney returned from his room with the Benjamins in a tight roll. He slid it toward Flores who fanned the large bills on the table. He handed the bunched bills to Luta. "Que es el total?" he said, without looking at the man.

"Està bien." The giant's resonance filled the room.

Satisfied, Flores sipped again. "And there is a question of weapons?"

Sydney nodded.

"That will be provided on the other side. Rafts have been known to overturn occasionally. No sense in losing valuable firearms."

The sooner the better for me, thought Sydney, *but . . .*

Noticing his reluctance, Flores said, "I assure you the selection will be quite extensive, Senor, and payment only when you are satisfied." His hands stretched toward Sydney. "You knew that was extra, of course."

Sydney smiled. "Of course."

Flores rose. Most of his small body had been hidden behind the table. Now, Sydney noticed a delicately embroidered shirt, primarily of white, gold and blue and a massive belt buckle of burnished bronze.

Sydney continued to survey the man. *Those boots must have cost thousands. He's higher up than I would have thought. The fact that he's not letting on might be a concern.*

Flores sipped the last of his coffee. He bowed to the group. "It has been a pleasure. My companions will see you across and I will see all of you at Los Ranchos." He followed the hulking Luta toward the door, then turned. "About your car?"

Sydney thrust his palms outward. "No use to us anymore."

Flores brow furrowed. "Is it traceable?"

"Only to a Nebraska man who died of influenza recently."

Flores nodded. "It is a better than the average car. We can change such vehicles remarkably well down here so that—and I know it doesn't exactly apply to a car—even their mother would not know them." He shook his head at the poor joke, clearing his throat. "Would a credit of five thousand dollars do—after all you cannot use it again."

"More than fair, Senor," Sydney said.

"Good." Flores walked out as Luta held the door. The knuckles of his massive hands were like walnuts. The scarred fingers jutted at odd angles.

This fellow has seen his share, thought Sydney.

Gilberto rushed over and thrust his head through the doorway. After calling "Adios, Senor Flores," multiple times in a progressively louder voice, he closed the door.

As they headed back to their rooms, Al-Musawi gripped Sydney's arm. "I do not trust that man."

"Nor do I," Sydney said.

Al-Musawi lowered his voice to a whisper. "I know these things."

"So do I," Sydney whispered back. "So do I."

CHAPTER 5 THE SAFE HOUSE

The two men standing at the entrance to the safe house appeared small but hard. As they approached, Gilberto gave them his usual jovial greeting. They merely grunted in response.

"Estan listos?" said one of the men, as if the three passengers weren't in the room. One of his eyes was nearly white, with a jagged scar running from below its center down to his upper lip. He wore a dirty white shirt and shorts that revealed bowed legs caked with mud.

"Yes," said Gilberto, nodding toward Sydney. "And that gentleman speaks Spanish."

"No me importa," was the man's gruff response. "I speak Ingles." The man turned toward Dalia, whose blond wig was back in place. "Rubia, are you ready?" he said with a protracted wink of his good eye.

"Yes," she hissed, glaring.

The man shrugged off her response. "I am Antonio and he is Rudolfo." The second man merely nodded. He sported a shirt with a Costa Rican tree frog that proclaimed *Pura Vida,* and shorts that resembled those of his partner. Unlike Antonio, his brown legs sparkled as if he had stepped from the shower. His oiled hair was slicked flat, strands sticking together like a floor mat.

"He does not speak English," said Antonio, "so you will leeson to my words at all times. For thees treep, I am the boss. Comprende?"

Sydney picked up his case. "Yes, we understand."

"Hokay. We are going to walk out the back door and a couple of hundred yards to the river. Eet ees dark and we can only use the moonlight, so stay close. Eet ees rocky and lots of leetle bushes, so be careful."

Gilberto hugged each of them as if they were family, before escorting them through the kitchen to the back door. There he hugged them again. As they set off he called after them, "Buena suerte."

Thanks, thought Sydney. *We'll need plenty of luck.*

***

"Rough" would hardly describe the terrain. The sand was uneven and prickly bushes grabbed at their legs. Making it all the more eerie were trees that *creaked* and *rattled* in the breeze. Next, they heard the river. A low whisper which became a ferocious *whoosh* as they approached.

Is it wide? Wonder how fast that's flowing. This is the heavy season. Sydney stood tiptoe to get a glimpse. There it was, broad and rushing, rippling and curling in the moon's rays. Occasional debris swept by like drowned bodies. Ironically, Sydney was aware the flotsam and scum could very well be decomposed body parts. The raft, able to fit at least eight, bobbed and bucked in the current.

"*Do not worry*," Antonio hollered above the rushing water, "*I theenk you say, 'thee bark ees worse than thee bite'. She ees easy to handle for us.*" He looked at Dalia with his good eye. "*We do thees easy. Don' worry.*" In response, she shot him a deadly glare.

Rudolfo, untying the raft from a gnarled stump, nodded in vigorous agreement.

"Thee suitcases first," said Antonio, reaching for Dalia's. "Good they are not large. Now the others." He handed them to Rudolfo who placed them toward the front. "And now, Senorita." He reached for Dalia's hand. She let him take it, then quickly yanked it away once she was in.

The two men got no such help. Each tottered before settling down on the pulsating rubber. Rudolpho, at the front, wielded a large paddle, as did Antonio in the rear.

The two Mexicans began to maneuver deftly against the current. Poised on the raft's spongy edge, Antonio looked down at them and said, "Thees river ees friendly to us who know it. Those who die are mostly the ones killed by the La Canicula. That ees the deadly heat during the summer. They are desperate fools who try during the day. Our only worry ees American border patrol—and they are too few to bother us—and they do not come so close to Nuevo Laredo territory. Too dangerous." A proud grin etched over his face as foam gusted and sprayed the raft.

He sounds like a bloody tour guide, thought Sydney. *Next he'll point out celebrity homes.*

"So you see, there is nothing to worry about," continued the one-eyed man. "And before you know eet, here we are." He spoke with the enthusiasm of a circus ringmaster. The raft bounced against the shore. Rudolfo leapt to the sand, tugging it after him.

Standing close to the rushing river, no one heard the sound of the *click* as the flashlight came to life in Antonio's hand. The grass and shrubs undulated under its powerful beam. Up in the distance, between the shadowy outline of trees, twin headlights blinked on and off.

"Come," said Antonio. "Bring the luggage. You are not coming back. I will help the senorita."

Dalia strode back to the raft. "I can take care of myself."

"Whoa–" Antonio's face curled in anger. "As you weesh, Senorita." He turned toward Rudolfo, who was about to loop the raft's rope over the dagger-like limb of a driftwood log. "The Senorita ees tired of our company. Vamonos, Rudolfo. Vamonos."

He turned to Sydney. "We are done. They weel pick you up here, gringo. Adios."

As the two slid the raft into the river again, a pair of high headlights bounded toward Sydney and his companions. The *throb* of a powerful engine competed with the raucous chorus of insects. A large pickup, tottering precariously upon oversized tires like huge donuts, suddenly loomed out of the darkness. Even idling, the vehicle's vibrations drowned out all other sounds. Through the driver's window, a high-pitched voice yelled, "Ven aqui, por favor."

Under the truck's doors were high running boards and steps. Once the group was settled, the driver, whose face was hazy in the dark interior, said, "Diez minutos hasta la casa."

"Ten minutes," said Sydney. "Bueno. Tenemos el equipaje."

The truck exploded onto the sandy soil, tilting and rolling as it crushed shrubs and small trees, bouncing off larger rocks like ball on a pool table. With every impact the powerful headlights splashed trees and sky before settling back to the business of illuminating the rugged ground.

All three passengers clutched side grips and seat fronts for dear life. Suddenly they were on a highway. In the beams, a sign proclaimed, "Rancho Penitas West." The driver cranked his gearshift and the vehicle quieted. Now it rode smooth as any luxury car. All they could see were occasional mobile homes, a few cabin-sized houses and fence stretching for miles. No more than ten minutes later, the truck stopped before a double gate. The right side of the gates swung open. In the lights appeared a man with a shotgun and a cartridge belt across his chest. He signaled them in.

"Hola," yelled the driver. "Porque no duerma, Paquito?"

The guard laughed and shot a finger. "Chinga tu madre, Luis," he called as the truck *crunched* along the gravel drive.

The house they came to was small, with sagging electric wires dipping into a box near the door. As they stepped down, a *snarling* erupted from deep in the shadows. The barking ended with a *yelp* as the *crack* of a chain pulled the beast up short.

"Puta!" yelled the driver into the dark. The dog whined and ceased to struggle.

Past the house, dark shapes of vehicles protruded indistinguishably. With *creaking* resistance the front door opened, leaving them blinking in harsh light.

"Come in." The speaker was invisible in the sudden glare as they walked up the two steps to the door. "Gracias, Jaime," said the man's voice.

"Si', Patro'n." Their driver drove off in a spray of gravel.

The man at the door shook his head. "That Jaime is loco behind the wheel." He ushered the three visitors in with a courtly flourish. "I hope he didn't make the trip too exciting."

"Just exciting enough," said Sydney.

Their host was tall and pale, with prematurely grey hair and pale blue eyes. His silk tropical shirt opened down to a large crucifix on his chest. "I am Senor Fuentes." His smile revealed an upper bridge of gold. "But since we are all friends, you may call me Don Pepito—a nickname with a long and boring history. Don Eduardo, who you met in Nuevo Laredo, sends his apologies, but I am to be your host now. Come, eat." He gestured toward a side table.

An array of fruits, cheeses and nuts sat on paper plates. "Drinks?" he inquired. "We have soda and tequila. I am sorry for the limited choices but, after all, this is just a temporary stop for you." The man tilted the tequila into a plastic cup. Curled worms floated to the bottle's surface as he poured.

Only Sydney accepted.

Don Pepito toasted him. "Now to business." He walked toward a table with six chairs. Its surface was bare except for a few ashtrays and a writing pad with an expensive Mount Blanc pen upon it. Apparently, during the ceremony over the food, two other men had silently seated themselves at the table. "These are my associates," the pale man said, without introducing them. "I am in a dangerous business and I never go without protection."

Sydney sat, his mind reading the circumstances. "Of course." *There have to be others. Now where would they be?* The room was long and narrow, with a kitchen alcove and three dark doorways. *Anywhere, unfortunately.*

"And the lady?" Don Pepito signaled toward Dalia. A large stone glittered as he waved her to a chair.

"Why not sit next to me?" said Sydney. "I like to keep her close." He laughed as his eyes met hers.

Don Pepito looked at his men, then shrugged. "I don't blame you, Senor. She is quite lovely. Yes, Rubias are my favorite." He bowed as Dalia seated herself. "Blondes. Very rare here in Mexico." His gold teeth radiated. He looked at Al-Musawi, who was still holding back near the door.

Al-Musawi waved off the invitation. "I have been travelling a long time. I will stand."

Sydney said, "Excuse my friend. He is very tired from travel—"

Their host spread his palms. Shards of fire flashed from his ring. "Of course. As he wishes." He leaned forward, crossing his arms. Age spots dotted his forearms. "Now, for the money, if you would be so kind."

Sydney removed the bills from his right pocket. *Just the right amount. And in the other pocket for the next items. None of their business how much else I have in the compartment in my suitcase.*

The pale man's long fingers delicately rifled through the bills. "Exactly correct. Thank you . . . and now there is a matter of weapons.

"Yes. Can you show us what's available?"

"Well, Senor Sydney, that would take a very long time." He smiled at his companions. "I don't suppose you are looking for missile launchers or military canons—these are quite popular with some of our African clients and," he nodded at Dalia, "some of your 'freedom fighters' soon, I imagine?"

Dalia stared at him without speaking.

"No," said Sydney. "Only semi-automatic weapons and side arms will do for this trip."

"Bueno," laughed Don Pepito. "One can only try." He nodded to one of his men, who stood and walked toward a closed door. Three knocks and it opened. Two men came out, each carrying two cases. From their slow movement and stooped backs, their burdens were obviously heavy. Each of them carried a revolver in their belt. They lifted the cases to the table with some difficulty, but did not open them.

Don Pepito's gold-toothed smile vanished. He stared at Sydney with eyes that were now nearly without color. "How much more did you bring, Senor? What you want is going to cost considerably more, even with," a giggle shook his narrow shoulders, "the discount for your car. Much, much more."

Sydney's hand went to his left pocket. "Of course, Senor. We aren't asking for charity." Under the table, his knee brushed Dalia's and she slid her chair away from the table. "Let me show you."

Don Pepito's smile was back, but his eyes remained cold. "Sure. Sure, Senor. It is always good business to lay our cards upon the table, as the Americans say." A spring-loaded pistol snapped into his hand. The barrels over and under it looked like tiny black snake eyes. "My advice about the weapons—it is best if you have much, *much more.*"

Instead of more money, a credit card appeared in Sydney's hand.

Don Pepito's eyes were wide with shock. "Ha, ha. You are going to pay us with a credit card? Ha, ha," he grinned up into the faces of the men holding the cases. His weapon slid sidewise. "Una tarjeta, ha, ha . . . "

A slash of Sydney's card left him blinking and bloody. The next instant Sydney ripped the tiny gun free of the blinded man's grip, and shot Don Pepito's grinning bodyguard standing above him before the astounded man could clear his weapon. The dead man sprawled forward. His brain and blood spilled over Don Pepito's writing pad and pen.

Unnoticed, Al-Musawi had positioned himself behind the man next to Dalia. Before the confused bodyguard could react, Al-Musawi thrust his left elbow beneath the man's chin, cupped it with his other hand and yanked upward. A harsh powerful *crack* cut off the dying man's scream.

The second man with a case in his hand swiped it at Sydney, knocking him sidewise.

Sydney's tiny gun skidded across the table, *clattering* to the floor. Drawing his weapon from his belt, the man with the case lunged for Dalia, but a throwing star pinched between her fingers slashed his neck. He clutched his throat but couldn't stem the blood pulsing from his carotid artery.

Swaying and gurgling indistinct words, he *thudded* onto the table, then slowly slipped beneath.

All eyes flashed toward the fifth man summoned by Don Pepito. He held a large revolver in his hand, but one look at his patron clawing at his sightless eyes sent him scrabbling back into the room from which he had come. The door *crashed* shut and within a moment, they heard the *screech of a window being jerked open.*

They waited. Except for Don Pepito's moaning, the house was silent. Even the dog outside was apparently asleep.

"Watch for the driver," said Sydney. He lit a cigarette and released the lid of the first case.

"What do I do with the blind guy?" Al-Musawi's deep voice was as offhand as if he was asking about taking out the garbage.

Dalia frowned. "Don't you know, Kassim?" Her question was answered by a resounding *crack.* The blinded man dropped to the floor. A subtle gleam of appreciation shot across Al-Musawi's face as he viewed the result of the same technique he had used mere minutes ago.

Sydney said, "Always play fair, Don Pepito." Then he turned to the contents of the first case. "Hmm, nice handguns. Take your pick ladies and gentleman and let's check inside and out."

Dalia hefted a Glock 9mm semiautomatic and grinned. "My favorite."

"I take the colt," said Al-Musawi.

"My choice, too." Sydney knocked a magazine into the chamber. "Let's check the rest of the place. Then find that driver and the runaway guy. I don't leave loose ends." He strode toward the next door, gun held ready. "Cover me, Musawi. I'll go low, you high."

The second door gave without resistance. They faced a vacant room. The third door yielded the same result. Sydney lowered his Colt. "Okay, let's see what other presents they brought."

The remaining cases yielded Uzis, AK47s and an RPG-7 grenade launcher. Every weapon sat there with full compliments of ammunition for it. As they collected their weapons of choice, Sydney said, "I hate leaving those H&K's and MP5's, but I think we're okay. Machine guns are overrated and hard to hide on your body. Take the other handguns and let's check out the grounds."

Fifteen minutes later they were sure the grounds were deserted. "Truck's there but the driver must have taken off with the other guy." Sydney snapped out his magazine and placed it in a pocket. "Plenty of cars. How about that Hyundai? It looks comfortable and I checked the gas. Full."

Dalia hurried back toward the house. "Sure," she said, opening the door. "I'm getting my things."

Within five minutes the car was idling before the door. Dalia lifted a plastic bag she had brought out of the house. "I couldn't let all that food go to waste."

Sydney's teeth glistened behind the headlights. "Good thinking. Now the mission really starts. Get in, my friends."

Overhead, a swollen, opal moon seemed to follow them.

CHAPTER 6 CHATTER

In a chic Washington restaurant, Senator Arlo Grossman sat devouring the last morsels of his coconut cream pie, a confection he had a notorious fondness for. His slender glasses perched atop his nose, offering a glimpse of his ever-alert, darting eyes. Amused colleagues on the Senate Committee on Energy often joked, "Better be quick if you want to catch Arlo's gaze."

At a youthful forty-one, Grossman was the youngest senator to lead a committee. Known for his unyielding dedication to Democratic ideals, his stronghold among Liberal supporters in Austin, Texas marked him as an unbeatable force, notwithstanding the bewildered reaction from other parts of the largely conservative Lone Star state.

Grossman's full face was tinged with concern. "This new president is aiming to extract every bit of oil shale, threatening to reverse decades of anti-pollution efforts. How did we miss his intentions?"

Reaching for a tiny pitcher, the sophisticated Hans Gerlinger, a Swiss figure linked to the local embassy, added a dash of milk to his tea. "He was never thoroughly vetted, I suppose. How could anyone have known?"

Worried about his committee's ability to counteract the impending changes, Grossman expressed, "We have to tread cautiously. The margin is slim. Many conservatives are drawn to the idea of 'energy independence,' disregarding the ultimate devastation to our planet." Gobbling up the last bites of his meal, Grossman revealed his concerns to Gerlinger about the potential impact on oil prices. "Perhaps the Russian Embassy could provide insight. Could you discreetly gather information?"

"Consider it done," Gerlinger assured, offering a reassuring pat.

**

Paris shimmered in the midday sun. Two handsome, dark men relaxed under a bright umbrella before a street-front café. Its windows boasted row upon row of delicate pastries mounted by swirls of lemon, mango and chocolate toppings. The heat didn't bother them and they were familiar with luscious desserts. Both, after all, were princes.

"You know, cousin," said the taller, "being ousted has its advantages." He lifted his champagne, examining the sunlight through its bubbles. His clothes were the latest in fashion. They always were.

"Agreed." The shorter man smiled and poured from the chilled bottle. "No more shapeless robes for state events and no more intrigues by the Sulimans. How many years now is it since we were booted out by our power-hungry cousin?" Before he could get an answer, he added, "I, for one, am glad." He lifted his glass. "Palace life is overrated. Most of the time I was bored."

The other man changed the subject. "You have better contacts in Riyadh than I. What is the word? Anything interesting?"

"Well." The shorter one leaned closer. "I understand that our prince and his inner circle are apoplectic about the new American president."

"Why?"

"Because the new president wants to bring back fracking."

The taller laughed. "Yes. Bless those Americans with their steam. Blow those rocks open again, dear Americans. Our families will be wealthy. Our equipment will be used again. Our natural gas investments will thrive again." He tossed down the golden remainder of his drink and refilled. "Damn our cousin and his oil. I'd rather get rich from American ingenuity—although I'm grateful for our allowances. Else, how could I live in gay Paree?"

"Yes," said the shorter. "The first thing my father did when that bastard banished us from the Kingdom was load up on those American companies. We were doing fine until—"

"The Democrats got back in," the other supplied. "I know. My Pioneer stock tanked the day after the election and continues the downward drop with all their clean energy nonsense. We've lost a fortune."

The shorter man shook his trimly bearded face. "So have we. Yet, if this information is true, now our investments could rocket."

The tall one nodded. "I hope the new president lives long and well."

"But—"

"What's the 'but,' Cousin?"

The short one signaled his companion closer. "I have heard there is a plot—"

"Not another?" laughed the taller.

"To destroy the new fracking."

"No? How?"

"I don't know . . . sabotage, I suppose."

The taller man's jaw dropped. "God. Bombs? Nuclear?"

"I don't know. That's all I could get. You know how secretive our rulers are—"

"And if this were true—"

"They'd never want the news out."

The taller man shook his head. "I like the Americans. I like the way they are. And I like the fracking money." He shook his head. "This is wrong on any account. How much death for a whole area? Maybe the world." Frowning at his glass, he set it down.

"Should I look into it further?"

"Of course, Cousin. This cannot be allowed . . . but be very careful." His shoulders quivered involuntarily. "You know what our king and the crown prince are capable of."

***

Although his official title was "Third Assistant Cultural Attache," Uri Spanov was no such thing. As it had transpired with many a former KGB officer, he, like Karmov, had reinvented himself, although not nearly as successfully as the Russian president. Still, he had Karmov's ear and a high rank in the intelligence arm of the Russian army, known among insiders as the GRU.

Like the Russian president, he was a fitness addict and wore shorts and bright red Addidas shoes for his weekly runs. His attitude was brusque, just like Karmov, and he despised the social niceties of embassy life.

He and Senator Grossman stood on one of the bridges spanning the wetlands of the aquatic gardens in D.C's

Kennilworth Park. They leaned upon the long rails six feet above softly undulating water lilies and rustling marsh grass. Darting dragonflies after their zigzagging prey were the only witnesses to this midday meeting. The park was a very popular spot for such "off the record" encounters.

Spanov glanced at his watch. "I do not have much time, Senator. I run here twice a week and stopping brings down my heart rate." Spanov's contempt for the out-of-shape man was apparent. The fact that Grossman was a Jew didn't help.

Grossman's feelings for the other man were no kindlier. "You're a well- known anti-Semite, Colonel Spanov—oh excuse me, Third Cultural Attache Spanov—so I'll get to the point. President Karmov isn't happy about our new president's openness to expanding drilling, I trust?"

Spanov shrugged. "Why do you say that? What does he care what you Americans do, as long as it doesn't threaten us?"

Grossman followed the flight of a darting mosquito. It landed on his wrist. He slapped but missed. It droned off. "I hate the outdoors, Spanov. And I despise the new President and his proposed environmental suicide. And I have many friends who feel the same. If I can be of help, let's say for any reason, get in touch. Texas is my turf, if you get my meaning. Now get on with your run." The overweight senator walked off without a goodbye.

Despite his cardio, Spanov took a long moment to consider the meeting. *He is an environmental fanatic with lots of power. This fool could be helpful, if he can be trusted. Unfortunately, we have such fanatics, too. But they are dealt with.* Spanov shook his head and laughed, expelling a gust of breath. *Only the West would coddle these idealistic fools. As my President says, they are soft and getting softer all the time.* He flinched at a darting dragonfly. *Well, I shall report this directly. There have been rumors—perhaps this can help. Never hurts the career, if it does.* With a deep whiff of the citrus-smelling lilies, Spanov thudded over the boards into the noon glare.

***

The Embassy of the Russian Federation in Washington is an unimaginative white structure broken up by rows of narrow windows.

Spanov's eighth floor office was similar to many others except that it was heavily soundproofed. The lower left drawer of his desk had a tamper-proof lock. Inside was a red phone, configured with a scrambler to repel all of the NSA's most sophisticated listening apparatus. The codes exchanged were also changed frequently to keep ahead of their adversary. Although not foolproof, the system worked well enough. Spanov reached into the drawer, and removed the device and his code book. The notations were in frequently erased pencil.

Karmov's voice was loud and clear. "Yes?"

"Sorry to interrupt, Mr. President—"

"Please, my schedule is brutal. What does the Main Directorate have for me today?"

Spanov took a deep breath. "I have heard that there may be ramifications from the change in leadership here."

Karmov's voice sharpened. "There are always ramifications."

"Well, if, and I say only 'if,' there is a contingency plan—"

"Stop being cute, Spanov." The voice over the phone could have cut through steel. "Whatever you have, get the fuck on with it."

Spanov's brow was sopping wet despite the blowing vent above his head. "A United States senator offered assistance—if such is necessary, and only if—"

"Shut up, Spanov! Whatever chatter you have heard or haven't heard, forget it *now!*"

"Yessir. Sorry.*" What the fuck have I done? You just can't tell with that man. He was always rude and egotistical but, as president, he is impossible.* The GRU officer was about to put down the receiver with a trembling hand when Karmov's shrill voice moved up an octave. "*Spanov.*"

"Yes, sir."

"Who is this particular senator?"

"Grossman is his name."

"And why is this particular senator of importance to me?" Karmov said.

"Because he is from their state of Texas."

"Ah. From Texas…with all the oil?"

"Yes, sir."

Karmov's voice softened. "Very good, Uri Ivanovic," Karmov switched back to the familiar. "Sorry—the affairs of state are taxing. Since you already suspect something, I will take you into my trust. *Do not violate it.*"

Spanov's back arched. "Of course not, Mr. President."

"You must arrange another meeting. You shall be

instructed as to its purpose. And not a word, do you hear?" The phone went dead.

Spanov swore at the instrument in his very best English expletives. "Arrogant fuck," he muttered before slamming down the receiver. Then he shut the drawer's elaborate lock with a decisive *click*.

CHAPTER 7 "IT'S MY BABY!"

After a restful night and a lackluster motel buffet, they started along I-35. The drive to Midland would be over six hours with little in between. Nearing the Laredo city limits, Sydney turned off I-35 where the sign said "Park Street."

Al-Musawi leaned thick arms over the front seat. "We just started."

"We need to change cars." Sydney concentrated on the turn. "The cartel knows what we're driving."

"Ah." Al-Musawi leaned back. "Just so."

A mile down, Sydney stopped. Near the corner of a side street a man was polishing the hood of a pristine Chevrolet. Sydney turned in, rolling down his window and said, "Looks like you keep it in pretty good shape."

The man stopped. He was in his 20s, thin, with tattoos along both arms. "It's my baby." His smile revealed a long gap between his front teeth. "Can't afford nothin' newer than a twenty ten, but ah keep it cherry."

The porch behind him sagged. Blisters on the sun-worn paint made the house look diseased. A sleepy hound hung halfway off of the top stair. An old rocker with cracked arms waited for pick-up at the curb.

Sydney cocked his chin at the tattooed man. "Come over and talk for a second. I might have something interesting for you."

The man thought it over, then walked toward their car. His smile was less certain. "Yeah? Don't try to sell me nothin'."

Sydney laughed. "No, I want to buy something. You interested?"

"Yeah, what?"

"Your car."

The man's eyes narrowed, "Why? Looks like yours is better'n mine."

"Good, Then how about a straight trade?"

The man walked the length of the Hyundai, then around the other side. "What's the catch?" he said as he approached the driver's side. "Is it hot?"

Sydney smiled. "Not locally. But a few changes would be in order."

The man bared his gapped teeth. "Not a problem. Straight trade?"

"Absolutely."

"You wait, I'll get my papers." The man almost tripped in his haste to get into his car. He flung open the glove compartment. Soon he was back brandishing a stack of papers. "Here's registration an' insurance. What else you need?"

"Nothing," laughed Sydney. "That will do. Keep the records but sign off on title—I'm sure you own it by now."

"Yeah, sure." The man scribbled his name. "It really runs well, ah promise."

Sydney began, "I think you don't need our papers—"

"Naw. Thet's fine. I'll get that little thing taken care of. Mah brother-in-law has a geerage. No problemo ."

"Can we use the driveway to transfer our belongings?"

"Aw sure. I'll bring mine in behind." He winked. "More private that way."

Sydney winked back. "Surely is."

Ten minutes later they turned back onto I-35 and Sydney said, "Believe it or not, this damn car drives better than the Hyundai."

CHAPTER 8 GROSSMAN AND GRISSOM

Mimi Grossman, an attractive woman of forty-six, was in as good shape as her senator husband was not. She pressed the button on the dishwasher and it respoinded with a *rumble*, followed by a *swoosh* of water.

"Arl, where are you going this time of night?" she said.

Their kitchen was less than typical. Arrayed along the walls were Mimi's prized collection of porclain wash basins, antique cutting boards and other paraphernalia dating back to her great grandmother's pioneering days. Her excuse, when challenged by her husband during the move to D.C. ten years ago, was that it reminded her of Texas. As usual, he had given in, although he considered it ridiculous in the compact chrome and steel mini-kitchen of their Washington apartment.

Arlo Grossman patted her hand. "You know the demands on a senator, dear. 'Neither rain nor sleet—'"

"Quit it, Arl, I've heard that one for twenty years." She frowned, following him past a green sectional sofa to the entrance of their apartment.

"Still applies, Sweetie. See you in a few hours. Then you can tell me what happened on *Dancing with the Stars*." He was out the door before she could respond.

Hours before, an aid had brought the senator a cryptic message: "How would eight next Thursday be to meet with campus activists. Rudy."

There was no "Rudy" and "next Thursday" was tonight. "Campus" was the Silver Diner in Falls Church Virginia.

After rush hour traffic, the drive would take about thirty-five minutes.

The shiny throwback to the 40s was crowded, as usual, but an end booth was available. Ten minutes later, a man came into view. The newcomer's hair was grey and a furry mustache covered his upper lip. Grossman hesitated to call out to the man when he noticed the thick-rimmed glasses and a Wizards tee-shirt. But the man's brusque voice and imperious manner soon convinced him that it was the Russian.

"You amateurs," whispered Spanov. "You act so surprised, Senator. Make a show of welcoming me as an old friend."

Grossman complied, going as far as trying to rise and hug Spanov.

"Enough," hissed the Russian. "Just sit!"

An Asian waiter appeared. "Fill up your coffee, sir?"

Grossman nodded.

"And you, sir? Here is a menu."

Spanov waved it off. "Just coffee."

Grossman said, "What's this about? Have you heard back? Do you need something?"

Spanov sighed. "Calmly, Senator. Calmly. And smile while I tell you. Even a little laugh wouldn't hurt, all right? And by all means, don't look shocked no matter what. Have you got that?"

I can't stand this bastard, thought Grossman, raising his cup to hide his feelings, *but, if he can help—*

Spanov read his mind. "I don't like you either." He smiled as if Grossman had just paid him a compliment.

"But we may be able to help each other, regardless."

"Yes. That's the important thing," Grossman agreed.

"You are familiar with the Permian Basin?"

Grossman's fleshy lips compressed. "Of course."

Spanov ignored the senator's hostile response. "And Eagle Ford?"

Grossman calmed himself. "Yes." His response was almost civil.

"Your biggest oil shale producers." Spanov didn't wait for an answer. "Could you help some colleagues of ours get access?"

Grossman pondered, then said, "I suppose."

Spanov smiled. "Do you want them stopped, or are you all talk, Senator? I understood that you were against new fracking. Am I right, or am I wasting our time? I can get up right now—"

Grossman leaned forward, tipping a napkin holder in his haste. "Yes. Yes, but I don't want anyone hurt. If I agree, you must understand that."

"Of course," crooned Spanov. "We don't either." He bent at the waist, whispering, "Just a little sabotage. No one hurt. But fires do happen . . . after hours." He looked hard at the senator although the glare of bright overheads reflected harshly from Grossman's glasses. "Of course, there may be some limited night staff . . ."

As was his habit, Grossman averted his eyes from the cold man's face. "Yes, I suppose . . ." He lifted his chest. "But *I insist* the danger must be kept to a complete minimum."

"Senator, I assure you, like yourself, we only desire to

destroy the fracking operation, not harm individuals. Fracking is a scourge to our environment as well as yours. The world still needs oil but certainly not this obscenity."

Grossman's eyes glowed behind his glasses. His hands gripped the table as he nodded again and again. "*It must be st*opped," he said too loudly. An elderly couple looked over from across the aisle. He smiled, shrugging and waving his open palms. "Sorry," he pantomimed. Facing Spanov again, his roundish face wore a smirk. "Although I'm unconvinced that your government's motives are as pure as ours. According to my sources, you haven't nearly the technology to institute fracking. Not for years." He waited for a response from Spanov, but the Russian's broad Slavic face remained impassive. "It must be stopped," Grossman repeated with renewed passion. "What do you need? I must be kept out of this, you know."

"Oh, of course, Senator. So must we. So must we. You might say we have the goods on each other, which is mutual assurance that we both keep each other's secrets." He thrust out his large hands. "That is why, we will be using outside intermediaries . . . little stupid pawns who, even if by some chance they are caught, will know nothing of either of us." Spanov slapped Grossman's shoulder, laughing as if they had just shared a great joke. Still smiling, the GRU man said, "We need details on the drilling operations. Types of equipment, locations, and methods of access. A senate aid—no need to know who— will leave the list of our needs under your rear wheel. When you have the answers, you will call the number on it. It is blind and untraceable. Someone will take the information."

Spanov rose. "I believe there is no need for us to meet again." He didn't extend his hand.

Good, thought Grossman, already fantasizing acre upon acre of burning gas without a single casualty. He ordered a sweet roll to dispel the distasteful Russian's former presence.

***

Ernie's bar in Midland was always packed during the fracking boom. Now business barely covered the rent and utilities. Ernie, a middle-aged man of average height whined to Harv Grissom, "If they hadn't killed frackin,' ah'd be a cunt hair away from retirin' now. 'Stead ahm serving guys like you who nurse a beer like it was a baby at your tit."

Harv Grissom waved a heavy knuckled hand at the proprietor. "Quit you're freaking whining,' you ol' has-been. You ain't nevuh gonna be able ta retire the way things is—an' if yuh don't quit cryin,' I'm goin' somewhere else an' there goes half yuh business raht there."

The daily dialogue between the two was pretty much the same since the energy boom had fizzled. Grissom's wife had just served him with papers and he was in no mood for the daily banter. He tipped the bottle of Lone Star past the three-day stubble above his upper lip. The face staring at him from the cloudy mirror behind the bar was shocking even to him. *What the fuck am I gonna do without Emma? Cain't blame her. Look'it thet kisser. I should be lying in the gutter with a gallon of buck-fifty vino. What the hell you doin', you reprobate? You used tuh make a*

hun'red-fifty bossin' fifty guys and Emma loved you. Sheet.
"How 'bout another, an' make it fast?"

Ernie Cosgrove put down a shiny glass. "Two fuckin' beers in a hour an' a half an' ahm supposed tuh jump. Fuck you." He walked toward a tub of ice in clumsy slow motion. Then he laid the bottle in front of Grissom, bowing. As his sleeve partially slid upward, a tattoo of a dagger dripping blood appeared on his powerful forearm. "Will the mastuh be wantin' anything else?"

"Yeah. Slide over them peanuts."

"Yuh eat maw goddam peanuts more than ah make on yuh sorry ass," grumbled the bar owner. A minute later the peanuts skidded toward Grissom. He grabbed a handful, spilling some.

Back to polishing his glasses, Ernie shouted "Will you fuckin' stop messin' up muh bar."

"Aint nothin' could mess up this shithole an' you know it." Grissom reached for his new beer. Frost dripped along his fingers. He stared at his nails. They were bitten down to the fleshy quick. *What the fuck am ah gonna do?* he asked the morose face in the mirror. *What?*

***

The road to Grissom's neat split-level was nearly deserted at 4 p.m. Some of the houses were boarded up. "For Sale" signs, as prevalent as porcupine quills, stuck up from lawns that hadn't seen a mower in months. It depressed Grissom as he made his way home in a slightly inebriated haze. He pulled his late model pickup into the drive and patted the wheel. *Bank'll be after this in a few months.* Booze could not lift his spirits as it had for the past year. *House is always dark now. She's with her maw, so get used ta it.*

Once inside, Grissom laid his Stetson on the kitchen counter. *Emma won't be telling me to git that off a' there, cause she won't be cookin' dinner no more, neither. Ah need me a fuckin' shower.* He was stripping when his cell phone rang. The upbeat tune angered him. *Gotta change that happy little ditty. Should'a done it long ago.* He applied his standard answer. "Yeah, which bill collector are you?"

The man on the phone sat in a small office in a Midland Texas high-rise. The office was so tiny that he could make it disappear within an hour, if necessary. The furniture was rented under an assumed name. The petroleum engineer credentials on the wall were fraudulent, his letterhead was a quick Kinko's job, and his roles changed as quickly as his assignments.

Being strictly freelance, he had no loyalties. He wasn't curious about who left the files in his post office box or why, as long as he could verify payment to his foreign account. The deposit showed up early this morning. He replaced his coffee cup and continued. "I assure you, if you are the man I need, you will have no trouble paying your bills. Shall we talk?"

"Ah got nothing but time."

"I've been told that you are very familiar with the oil fields, shale as well as crude."

"Bet yuh ass. Fifteen years in the business before the Washington assholes shut us down. Who my talkin' to?"

The man behind the desk frowned. "Ask that again and

our business is over."

"Okay." Grissom fought back panic. "No more questions. Ah git it. No more questions. Sorry."

"Good. Now, in a day or two, if I approve, you will be meeting with a team. They are international experts doing a study on the feasibility of reopening operations in the Permian."

"Hell, that's great news!"

The voice continued as if Grissom hadn't spoken. "These experts represent foreign investors and this is highly confidential."

"Yeah, ah git it. Competition an' stuff."

"Exactly. I am relieved that you understand. You are obviously a discreet man and your fee would be commensurate. This is a *very* big deal, if you get my drift."

"Sure. And what might the fee be, suh, if I may ask?"

"In the neighborhood of twenty thousand dollars for three days, plus reinstatement with the new company at twice your prior salary . . . *if* you are the right man."

Grissom's palms were so damp that he feared the little phone might slip from his grasp. "Oh, ah am. Why ah know everythaing 'bout the Permian. Ah really do."

"Even water sources?"

"Hell, yeah . . . uh, suh. All a' 'em. Cain't frack without th' water."

For the first time the man behind the desk smiled. "You are certainly right, Mr. Grissom. I think you're the man we need—but extreme secrecy is essential. One word and you won't be the right man. Am I understood?"

"Ah'll be the—whadda they say—soul a' deescretion."

"Good. Good. I think this will be a very good relationship. As a token of belief in you, you will find a large envelope in your mailbox—"

"Wha . . . how'd ya know where—"

"I said we are very thorough, Mr. Grissom. Please don't doubt that and don't interrupt again. As I was saying, it will be in your mailbox by morning. Don't worry about how . . . and give it to the people who contact you, *unopened*. My people will be in touch very shortly. Goodbye."

"Yeah, a very good relationship," echoed Grissom, but the line was already dead. In his shower, Grissom sang *Yellow Rose of Texas* and fantasized about Emma coming back to a newer and bigger house with a king-sized pool. "She'd like that," he said aloud.

CHAPTER 9 THREATS AND LEADS

Candlelight reflected against a bay window high on Montmartre. Beyond, the great dome of Paris's Sacré-Coeur basilica pinked in late sunlight. Grey haze already obscured its smaller twin domes.

The tall Saudi prince toasted his beautiful guest as a servant laid chilled cups of vichyssoise before them. "I hope my chef's soup is half as delicious as you are beautiful, Chèri." The rental wasn't overly opulent, but just comfortable enough to entertain a few dinner guests. He'd taken it for the view which showed through the floor-to-ceiling windows. All of the rooftops and lit windows of Paris lay below.

"And ah 'hope eet ees as good as you are charming, Mon tresor."

This is going well, thought the prince, when his cell phone *jangled. Did I not*

turn that damn thing off? He reached to silence it when he recognized the number.

"Please excuse me, Chèri. It is my cousin." He smiled through his displeasure." Business you know."

He rose and walked to his den. "Couldn't you have waited till tomorrow, Ali? You know this is the night—"

"No." The answer was firm. "Not this, Cousin."

"Is it about—"

"Yes, exactly."

Prince Ahmed's dark eyes hardened. "What is the news?"

"Bad, Cousin. A foolish minister of the Prince's, one of his untalented family of hangers-on, just had to brag. He's known for it. He told my contact that *very soon the Americans will be too busy filling hospitals to pursue the new president's wishes.*"

"Where?"

"Texas. The Permian. A virus that spreads and spreads."

"When, Cousin . . . and how? Tell me."

"I know there is a team already on its way and it includes those Hezbollah maniacs—this is right up those crazies' alley. What a disaster they made of Lebanon. This gossiper is proud because everyone thinks that China and India will buy oil cheaper from the United States if production increases again. He says those Iranian fanatics are also involved. I, myself, wouldn't be surprised if the Russians were, too. They would lose billions if Germany and the EU went for American energy, instead."

Ahmed stared at the Paris lights below. "Sure, it's cheaper and cleaner. That's why we invested. This is— forgive me, Cousin, I know you hate the expression— fucking awful."

"In this case, it is, Cousin. It *really* is."

Ahmed stared at the lovely girl. She looked back at him and pantomimed yacking on an imaginary phone. Normally he would have laughed. This time he merely signaled with an upraised index finger and a blown kiss. "I took courses from a guy who taught at Midland College in Texas. He was a petroleum expert at the Professional Development Center."

"You?" laughed Ali. "When did you find time to study with all those Yellow Roses of Texas?"

"Before we were ousted, dear Cousin, my father had plans for me to be our county's leading oil authority. He said I could be the next minister, if I studied." In his fury at the missed opportunity, Ahmed squeezed the phone hard. It uttered a frantic *bleep*.

"Ahmed. Ahmed!"

"Sorry Cousin, I'm still here. Anyway, you know where those plans went." He waved two fingers at the girl. "So, instead, all I do is eat well and make love . . . not a bad trade off—"

"I know. We all had bigger plans. Well, things could be worse. There is always the Mabahith to make arrests and lock the victims in their cozy dungeons, so . . ."

"I know. Some are never seen again when spirited away. Anyway, that's too depressing for a candlelight dinner."

Blurry haloes surrounded the candles in front of the girl. Ahmed rubbed the heel of his hand against his right eye, clearing his vision. "I talked to my professor friend there a few months ago. He's a good man and may know what to do." Ahmed took a long breath. "I should, shouldn't I?"

"Yes, Ahmed. It's the right thing to do and we don't owe Prince Suliman anything but grief." Ali laughed the silly giggle that Ahmed knew from childhood. "Now, get back to your evening business. Have you pointed out the view from your bedroom?"

"After the food, dear Cousin. We will get there after the

food."

***

Sydney and his team drove along one of Midland's main roads. Neon signs exploded their messages through the sultry night air.

"Can we go sightseeing?" laughed Dalia.

"I think we just did," said Al-Musawi.

Dalia whirled toward the back seat. "Why, Hashim, you made a joke."

"I know how to be funny, but it was unintended." Al-Musawi glared. "Just turn around, woman. Our mission is too important for jokes. Jokes are for idiots unless we are back at home celebrating our mission. Jokes can make us fail."

She turned away. "All right, all right. I didn't mean to insult you. Sorry. Look, there's a motel, Sydney." She pointed toward a plain brick building with a green sign. "Quality Inn. Okay? I'm dying for a bath."

"Paah, a bath." Al-Musawi was still out of sorts.

Dalia couldn't resist. "*You* should take one."

"I am clean, but I take showers, not little sweet-smelling baths."

"Enough," said Sydney. He was calm but icily firm. "We're all tired. Take your baths or showers—I don't care which--and we'll eat and get some rest. Tomorrow our mission begins. Got it?"

Both passengers answered affirmatively in weary voices. There was something formidable they sensed about Sydney that warned them not to antagonize their otherwise congenial leader.

After a mediocre meal at a national chain, Sydney parked at the motel. "You go in. I have to make a call. Sleep well."

He pressed a local number into his glowing phone and spoke when the call was picked up. "We've arrived, Cousin Saul. How are you and Aunt LuLu?" The code was simple but clear.

The man in the small office had picked up the call on the second ring. "Auntie can't make it but her friend, Harvey Grissom, will be at the Midland Diner at eleven. He'll be wearing a blue shirt saying 'Pioneer Drilling' and will have a series of plans which should help. He also has years of experience in the Permian and thinks that you represent Middle Eastern oil investors getting information for a huge fracking start-up. He has been properly incentivized to help you in any way, namely a high paying supervisory job and many benefits. I trust you know your role. Good luck. Auntie and I will see you for dinner, Friday."

'Friday.' Typical middle-man asshole, thought Sydney, pocketing his phone. *That means bugger off and don't call again. We take the risks and these turds sit nice and safe and get paid for practically nothing. They may not make as much but they can run ten of these operations at the same time to my one. Still, who'd want to sit on their ass in some office? I love the action, myself. And, of course, it pays a bit more.*

With the same abundance of caution which had kept him alive over the years, Sydney was about to drop the phone in the trash but thought better of it. He hadn't used his conventional "dumb" phone, which couldn't be tracked by Wi-Fi or Android but, also, wasn't reusable, because a variation of his original plan was germinating in his fertile mind. Sydney pocketed the instrument and pulled out the key-card to his room.

***

Captain Davey Stedmier sat in his office in Texas Ranger headquarters. He was a tall, lean man of thirty-two, with sun-leathered skin due to his propensity to prefer the field, whenever possible. This, despite being on the fast-track toward becoming the youngest ranger major ever.

Stedmier stared at flowering shrubs that separated the building from Austin's busy route 183, but he wasn't evaluating traffic. The call from his friend at Midland College had unnerved the decorated ranger. Any threat to the West Texas oil fields was bound to.

The ranger reviewed his notes on the sketchy conversation with Artie Krause, a revered lecturer at the college's Petroleum Professional Development Center. Krause's credentials were a mile long and he and Stedmier had thwarted a plot by organized crime to take over a wildcat drilling company six years prior. Krause's analysis of irregularities in the company's financials had put the nail in the coffin. Since then, the two had become fast friends and Krause had proven invaluable to the ranger's organized crime probes on multiple occasions.

However, this was different. This time it was Krause who tipped off Stedmier. The information from a former student suggested possible sabotage of the Permian fracking operations. Many of the young captain's closest friends were devastated by the sudden fracking shutdown two years before. More than one suicide was attributable to the desperation of proud men forced into unemployment.

It wasn't our way, thought Stedmier. *Texans would rather die than take charity. Now thet things'ull be bettuh, someone wants ta destroy the hopes a' thousands a good people again.* A sharp *crack* startled him. Stunned, Stedmier stared at the pencil bent perpendicular between his thumb and index finger. *Not on my fuckin' watch.* He speed-dialed the number of the El Paso Ranger Division. "This is Stedmier. Tell yuh captain ah need ta see him today. Ah'll be there as soon as ah can."

***

"Mr. Krause?" asked the puzzled young man who stood before Artie's lectern.

The lecturer looked up at the young man with a lost look in his eyes. "Oh, sorry, Mr. Samuels, my mind was wandering." *Sure is,* thought Artie Krause, *when the Permian Basin could be the target of who knows what? Bad enough we've lost gas production with all those damn executive orders. Thank God we have a sane man back in office now, but what if it's stopped again?*

And what if Ahmed has it only half right? What if all oil is shut down by these fanatics? More foreclosures, more suicides, mass migration? This area would lose half the population and all the businesses which are dependent on them, just as we're coming back.

Artie's mind's eye saw new acres of homes boarded up and decaying; closed schools and shopping centers—

"Mr. Krause?" The eyes of the freckled young man, a

talented prospect in petroleum economics, squinted with concern beneath a wrinkled brow.

"Sorry, Mr. Samuels." Krause smiled. His chubby cheeks surrounded his very bright, very blue eyes. "Yes, the ratio of expenses to capacity to world market prices is always primary."

"Taking into account fluctuations."

"Quite so," the lecturer answered. "The anticipated price fluctuation curve. I'd say you have it."

The young man beamed. "Thank you, sir. Next week?"

"Next week," said Krause and fist-bumped Samuel's shoulder. Loaded down with source books, the young man trundled off.

How many 'next weeks?' thought Krause while he slowly gathered up his materials. He turned for a moment and surveyed the empty lecture hall. It was large, with many tiers of seating. Krause's lectures were always packed with young people aspiring to make a name in Texas' fabled industry. A wrinkle creased his forehead. *How many of those seats will be filled if Ahmed is right?"*

***

"Where's the Captain, ranger?"

The young man wore the customary tan uniform with a blue tie. His ten-gallon cast shadows over his eyes but the strong jaw and clean chin were still visible. Over the left pocket of his shirt rode a five-pointed star. The customary boots were hand embroidered and obviously expensive. *Must have been a gift,* thought Stedmier. *He's not affordin' those on a startin' ranger's salary.*

The young man snapped to attention with military

precision. "The Captain is in his office, sir. I'll take you there."

"No worry, ranger. Ah know the way real well. Thanks."

"Well, well, how ya doin', Davey. "Ain't seen yuh in, le'see , more n' a horney armadillo's mating cycle, right?"

Despite his concerns, Stedmier had to grin. Captain Tobey Flynn was as jovial as law enforcement would allow. More than once he had suffered a Flynn "hot foot," or been red faced at meetings from a Whoopee Cushion. Still, nobody could stay mad at Flynn. "He's too damn entuhtainin' in a serious business," was Stedmier's standard defense of his friend. "You'd know more about armadillos' sex lives than ah would, Toby. How's it goin?'"

With a heavy *slap* on the shoulder, Flynn escorted him in. The view from the fourth story overlooked much of the El Paso landscape. "Take a seat, Davey." His forehead rose. "This ain't no social call?"

"Fraid not. We might have a situ-ation."

Flynn whipped out a pack of Wrigley's. Offered it. When Stedmier declined, he slid out a stick, nodding for his friend to begin. Ten minutes later, his thick lips had compressed and deeper furrows lined his brow. "Yuh sure a' the source? This could be a hoax."

"Yuh know Ahtie Krause, right? Do yuh think he wouldn't be convinced that it was credible before calling me?"

"Yup, ol' Artie sure 'nough would be." Flynn spat his gum into its silver wrapper, balled it up and shot it at a basket across the room. It wasn't even close.

"Yuh have a basket nexta your desk, Toby."

"No challenge." Flynn hefted his bulk out of an old swivel chair that *shrieked* every time he shifted his weight. At fifty-two and rather bulky, he was surprisingly light on his feet. He bent. Scooping up the shiny ball, he flipped it into the basket.

"When ya gonna retire thet funky chair?"

Flynn wiggled back down causing an exceptionally grating *squeak.* "When ah retire. 'Betsy' an' me are here fuh the long haul." Per his reputation, Flynn could go from humor to dead seriousness, instantaneously. "So, Artie knows this informant since the guy was a student. An' the guy's an A-rab?"

"Yup. A deposed royal."

"Yeah." Flynn shook his head. "Down ta his las' twenty million."

Stedmier rubbed his chin. Stubble was already emerging. "So, if there was a team heading in, how would they do it? Not Laredo?"

"Nah. Not over the bridge. They'd slide in over the river, more'n lahkly. Our fren's in the Nuevo Laredo Cartel would be glad tuh help fer a price. Them Arab terrorists and those cartel boys have worked more'n one deal, don'tcha know?"

"Anythaing turn up lately?"

Flynn snapped his fingers. "Shit, yeah. Shit, yeah, ah say. Yestiday, down by the Ranchos." His eyes narrowed. "Yeeeah. That fits. Buncha bodies in one a' them houses the cartel uses for droppin' off high payin' folks in a hurry to enter our fair land. The ones who don't wanna be seen sneakin' crossin' with the ordinary clowns pourin' over our bordah. Deal musta' gone real bad. They overcharged the wrong boys. Houses are far apart but a neighbor heard the dog barkin' fuh twenty-four hours straight. One of the deceased was Don Pepito, a major player. The others wuh th' usual assholes."

"Only a trained team could'a done that."

"Mighty well trained," agreed Flynn, "takin' out a buncha' those boys. An' my guys found lots'a weapons. First class stuff—"

"That means they're well-armed," said Stedmier. "Sheet."

"Sheet is right," said Flynn. "An' there was a bunch'a cars. You bet they got one."

Stedmier shook his head. "No chance a trackin—"

"Cartel cars," laughed Flynn. "Hell no."

Stedmeir sat back, thinking. He pulled out a pouch of chewing tobacco, inserted a pinch between his teeth and began to lightly chew so as not to break up the leaves. "Safe to assume they're heading for the Permian."

Flynn also settled back. A piercing *squeal* emitted from his ancient chair but he hardly noticed. "Yeah, outta Laredo, you take fifty-five ta ten. Easy six hours or so ta Midland."

Stedmeir thrust upward. "Ah got changeovers in muh trunk. Always deep 'em an' they ain't too funky yet. What say we go call on ol' Ahtie at the college? It ain't about financial conniving, like he specializes, but that boy shore knows the Permian, too. Might give us a clue ta' what a bunch'a terrorists would be after out thet way."

CHAPTER 10 THE CON

Grissom toyed with the idea of ordering another Lone Star when a tall, bronzed man approached him. "May I join you?" the stranger asked.

"Am I expecting you?" Grissom's response was calculated, following the instructions he had received. He had chosen a secluded booth at the rear of Ernie's based on a phone conversation, though the place wasn't particularly crowded. Grissom gestured toward the seat opposite.

Sydney quickly sized up the man: a two-week-old beard, a crumpled Astros shirt, and eyes tinged with redness and lines at the corners. He noticed dust swirling beneath the yellowing fan and caught a faint whiff of spilled beer as he checked the bench before taking a seat. Grateful that Grissom hadn't suggested a more upscale restaurant, Sydney maintained a polite smile. He flipped out a Hetfield and offered the box.

"No thanks," declined Grissom. "I've pretty much quit."

"Good for you," Sydney responded, taking a drag of his cigarette and letting the smoke waft toward the ceiling. "Too much tension in my business to be able to quit."

Hope gleamed in Grissom's eyes. "You work in oil?"

"As I'm sure our contact informed you, yes. I represent significant interests in the Middle East. We're seeking to launch an operation, but we need someone to help choose the right location and team."

Overcome by hope, Grissom blurted out, "I can do it. I'm your man, believe me."

Sydney played along. "Well... we know about your credentials from our local contact—"

"Yeah, yeah," Grissom interjected. "Many years of experience, from my early days." He chided himself mentally, realizing he was coming off too desperate. "Of course, the terms need to be right."

Sydney took a long puff, nodding deliberately. "Naturally, for a man of your experience—"

"Yes, experience," Grissom emphasized, clenching his fists. "That's the bottom line."

"Mr. Grissom—"

"Call me Harv."

"Sure, Harv. What my principals need to see is the whole layout of this area. The Permian Basin is vast, and to make a decision—"

"Yeah, yeah, you need to get the lay of the land." Grissom mentally scolded himself for interrupting. *I've got to stop butting in, but that darn beer on an empty stomach...*

Sydney didn't seem fazed by the interruption. "Precisely. You seem to grasp our needs remarkably well." This fellow is grinning like I've given him a medal, Sydney observed. If Grissom is as knowledgeable as he is gullible, we've struck gold. "My team includes a man and a woman from the conglomerate, but they lack familiarity with this country. You'd need to account for that—"

"Of course, sure. It's a big country and all new to them." *Harv, will you stop cutting in, you fool? That beer on an empty stomach was a bad idea.* "And I've worked with folks from there before. Really good people."

Sydney's lips widened into a smile. "Glad to hear that. Wouldn't work otherwise. Can we pick you up here around two?"

"There's an egg place nearby. I'd like to grab a bite."

Sydney stubbed his cigarette into an empty bowl with a few nuts scattered around. *At least he had nuts for breakfast.* Maintaining his smile, he rose. "Sure, tell me where."

CHAPTER 11 FRACKING ANYONE?

Artie Krause's office wasn't at the Petroleum Center, but in a large high-rise farther down Main Street. Its luxury was concomitant with his stature as one of the country's leading petroleum authorities. Through large windows, a blush of afternoon sunlight painted the walls donning rows of plaques and awards. As the rangers gaped, Krause said, "I guess you boys have never been up to my new office. Well, don't let that crap on the walls bother you. It's just to impress the corporate big shots that need to feel important."

He nodded toward an adjoining room with a long conference table, multiple matching chairs and three huge hanging monitors. "That set-up costs a fortune—all for show. These characters couldn't decide on a sandwich if it weren't presented on charts and in full color."

Stedmier shook his head, laughing. "Damn, Ahtie, yuh may be a learned man, but yuh as down ta earth as any ol' boy ah know. An' tha's sayin' something for—no offense—a New Yorker."

Flynn shifted in his chair and his eyes widened. He didn't know Krause as well as Stedmier did and wasn't sure how Krause would respond.

"Taken as a compliment from a Texas redneck," Krause replied.

Both Stedmier and Krause laughed.

Flynn squinted, staring at one, then the other. All of the sudden his cheeks squeezed upward toward his eyes and he, too, laughed. "Might as well join in if'n you boys ah gonna tear inta each other thet way. Don' leave me outta it."

Krause walked toward the conference room. "Might as well use the damn thing since I'm paying a fortune for it. Come on in." He produced a Jack Daniels and three glasses and filled each half-way. "You boys don't mind a little bourbon? It's after hours."

"Suits me fine," said Flynn, reaching for a glass. I do my best sleuthin' aftuh hours."

Stedmier lifted his. The brown liquid glowed ike late afternoon sunrays. "You do your *only* sleuthin' aftuh hours."

All laughed, toasting one another. Then it got serious.

Stedmier placed his glass on an orange "Hook 'em Horns" University of Texas coaster. "If these guys are on their way—"

"Or already here, Sted," corrected Flynn.

"Yeah, or already here. How would they best destroy fracking?"

"Or *all* Permian production, including oil," added Krause, steepling his hands against his nose. "That there *is* the question."

***

"Thees is where thee signals are from." Panchito Herrera squinted at the Laredo Street signs.

"Si'. Thee next block, I theenk." A very big man with a long handlebar mustache held his phone in a thick hand. "Near thee corner, Panchito. There eet ees." His stubby index finger pointed at the Hyundai. "That ees one of Don Pepito's." He genuflected. "God rest hee's soul. I even drove eet to make un delivery once. Hey, but the paint…Claro, they changed eet. And that trim. Muy feo. Terrible color. But I do not doubt eet ees ours. Thee leetle tracker never lies. ”

"I see. Yes, I see." Panchito rolled his eyes as he parked across from the Hyundai. *My big amigo ees not so bright, but strong. Yes, very strong.* "Those putas are not very smart. Don't they know we monitor all our autos to see that no driver runs off with thee merchandise. Que estupido!"

Big Pancho slid out the magazine from his automatic, then slapped it back in. "They will soon learn how stupid, hey Panchito. Ha, ha, ha." His deep-throated laugh filled their Jeep Cherokee. "Once we cut off their balls and feed them to them."

"Big Pancho, you stay here. You are too noticeable. I will evaluate. Watch for my signal." The smaller man pulled on a raincoat, heavy for the extreme heat, but it had another purpose. Its inside pocket was designed to hold a long machete: his weapon of choice. He walked to the house.

The porch sagged under his weight. *Sheet, this puta may collapse any fohcking minute.* There was a growl that ended in a cough. Panchito spun, hand reaching under his coat. *Oh, fohck! An old dog.* The hound looked at him. At the bottoms of its sad, rheumy eyes was an inch of pink flesh.

Ehh, how ugly. The Mexican fingered his weapon, but the dog merely wagged its tale. Then its heavy head sank down upon its paws. In a moment, it was sleeping.

"Yeah?" An unexpected face in the doorway startled Panchito. "What?" The man surveyed Panchito's long coat, then the gold earring in his right ear. "What kin ah do fer ya, amigo?"

Call me "amigo," motherfucker. I'd kill you just for that. Panchito's smile was practiced and quite perfect. "Please escuse, pero el coche." He pointed at the Hyundai. "Es muy bonito."

The man's smile revealed multiple dark spaces between his teeth. "Ah just got it. Glad yuh like it."

Thees gringo is ugly. "You got eet aqui?" Panchito pointed toward the ground.

"Yeah."

"I," Panchito pointed at his own chest, "like one. Where you get?"

"No, no, fella. Someone, how do you say, 'traded,' sheet how do you say—"

"Thee word is 'traded,' stupid!" Panchito looked back at Big Pancho. No one else was on the street. He, nodded, then turned, sliding out the machete and placing its point against the man's skinny chest. "Get inside, *Amigo*. I have some questions."

Big Pancho turned off the ignition and strode toward the house.

***

Before rejoining Grissom, Sydney decided to turn in the Chevy at one of the lots on Midland's used car row. "We can't take a chance on this car anymore. One never knows who's checking up," Sydney explained, as they pulled into Big Bart's One Thousand Percent Satisfaction Auto Corral.

Bart, himself, was significantly shorter than the name of his business.

"His belt buckle alone could give him a hernia," whispered Dalia as the diminutive man approached.

Sydney had to grin. *This lady, who kills so easily, has quite the sense of humor. Seems we're all filled with contradictions. Aren't people complex?*

The diminutive man wore a string tie and a huge hat that rested on his ears. His mouth barely made it up to Sydney's open window. "Howdy, I'm Bart. I may be small but my deals are *huge!*"

As if he hadn't used that line a thousand times before. Sydney couldn't resist. "Where's the accent, Bart?"

The little man's lips compressed in an unhappy frown. "To my everlasting shame, I was born in Ohio." Suddenly his lips curled upward. "But I'm a Texan at heart, pod'ner. What can I do you for?"

"We want to trade—"

"Trade? Did you say trade? Why I may be small but my trades are—"

Dalia leaned out the window. "Don't tell me . . . Huge?"

"That's right, lovely lady. Hee-uge."

After twenty minutes of haggling over their— suddenly—"mighty old" Chevy, the team drove off in a 2014 Honda Civic. Sydney offered to pay the difference in cash as long as Bart made it fast.

"No problem." The little man had winked after offering Sydney a large cigar. "All of us boys along the row make accommodations for good customers."

Sydney had told Bart to keep the cigar before they left for the airport.

"Why the airport?" asked Dalia. "We don't have a lot of time."

Sydney lit a cigarette, careful to blow the smoke out his window. "We need a luxury model. We represent wealthy interests. This car would never do, but we may need it once we're done with the operation."

Dalia's dark eyes wandered over Sydney's face. *What a nice profile he has.* Then she leaned toward him. "Got another cigarette and a light, Sydney?"

***

Grissom was outside a restaurant whose streaked windows hadn't been washed in months. When he saw their big rental Mercedes, his sleepy eyes nearly doubled in size. He nervously dusted his jeans before folding down the auxiliary seat facing Dalia. "Wow, you guys travel in style, don't yuh?"

"This is nothing compared to what we ride in back in . . . well, back there," said Sydney.

"Oh, ah git it,' said Grissom. "Cain't reveal the location a' your people. Ah git, it."

"Yes," said Dalia. "Mr. Grissom, you are absolutely right. Competition, you know."

"Oh yeah. Ah git it. You can call me Harv." He fixed his eyes on Dalia as if mesmerized.

Her smile glowed with promise. "Sure, Harv. Call me . . . Chris."

Sydney and Al-Musawi exchanged looks in the front. Sydney half turned. "Okay, you two, break it up. It's time for business. Where do we go? Harv."

After only a few minutes, the Mercedes was standing

before a large lot filled with vehicles. "It looks like a bloody parking lot,' said Sydney.

"In a way, it is. Let's drive in. Ah know the guys. Pioneer's the biggest, but fracking operations pretty much all look the same."

A big man in jeans and an orange vest walked over. He stared at the stretch. When Grissom rolled down his window, he said, "Grissom you sonofabitch, you find your own well?"

"Not yet, Mike, but ah got hopes. Just wan'na show some frien's aroun'.'"

Mike waved a fleshy arm. "Go ahead. Ain't gon'na be much happening till things kick up in a few weeks. See ya."

"See ya," said Grissom and turned to Sydney. "Go over there," he pointed. "We'll work our way around. Do any of yuh know frackin'?"

Sydney turned back to the man. "Well, you inject water into shale and it blows up into shale oil and gas."

"Hey, not bad," said Grissom. "Not bad a'tall."

"We've got a lot of money at stake here, Harv. We did our homework, but we've never seen the equipment in action. That's why we need you."

"Okay, then. Le's start with that red thing popping up, lookin' like a little tower. Thet's the well head. Ever'thaing goes down there, an' the gas and oil come up from there when the process is done."

"So that is the top of the well?"

"Yeah, but it's not like a regular well thet goes straight down. This one is drilled part down then takes a sharp angle so's they kin take what they want from nearby areas without re-drillin'. Called di-agonal drillin'.'"

Dalia smiled at the man. "Sounds like you get more bang for your buck, right Harv?"

"Tha's right, lovely laduh. 'Spensive ta drill a well. Cheaper ta use one well 'stead of a bunch.'"

"So one pipe goes down and bends to cover a greater area?" Al-Musawi's voice showed more enthusiasm than Sydney could remember thus far. "All over."

"Yeah, all the hell over," Grissom agreed, as if Al-Masawi was a curious child. "Now, the main thaing they pump down under pressure is watuh from them tanks." Grissom pointed at row upon row of black cylinders which towered over the huge trucks next to them. "Biggest ones are ta catch the water flowin' back. It's messy an' the county raises hell if' any gits back inta the drinking water supply."

Dalia batted her eyes. "This is fascinating, Harv. I know about our oil production, but this is new to me."

Grissom's face pinked beneath his three-day stubble. "Yeah, well, ya gotta be in the business. It's complicated."

"Oh, I know."

All right. Don't lay it on too thick even for this fool, thought Sydney. "We've got a lot to learn in a short time, *Dalia.* Go on please." He spurred Grissom on, as he shot a hard look at her.

"There's stuff they mix with the water. See thet monster truck. Tha's the sand." He pointed to a very long dump truck. "Thet sand an' water balls up down there an' plugs the fissures in the broken up shale. Thet's so's the gas an' oil under pressure don' escape afore they make it up ta the surface."

Sydney rushed on to prevent anymore of Dalia's ridiculous flirting. "What about all those other trucks with the big equipment on top?"

"Them there are the pumps ta force the water down under high pressure. Without that, the water wouldn't be strong enough ta break up the shale. An' there," the Texan pointed to another very long truck bristling with tank-like structures, "is also where otha chemicals are mixed in ta help the whole thang happen. Called the 'Blenda'."

"*Blender*," blurted Sydney. He regretted it immediately.

Grissom's face reddened. "Shore. 'Blenda'. Ain't thet what ah said?"

"Sure, Harv, that *is* what you said." Sydney pointed to a monster vehicle with tanks sticking out all along its top like fat quills with the intention to distract the man. "What is that giant there?"

Grissom warmed. "Yeah, that's a big boy. Well, when the stuff comes up its all gooey from sand an' oil an' chemicals, an' all the other crud from the earth, so it's gotta be sep'rated. The good from the bad. Or it ain't gonna do nobody any good."

"So that's a Separator," Dalia said. Her eyes sparkled with superbly feigned surprise.

Grissom looked at her and saw the delicate pouting of her mouth. "Give the little lady a 'A,'" he crowed. "You sure getting' the hang a' this. You sure ya never been 'roun' frackin'? You' a natural."

Sydney exchanged a glance with Al-Musawi.

The big terrorist's lips curled as if there were a bad

smell in the car.

Sydney kicked the side of Al-Musawi's shoe in warning. "Well, Chris has had a lot of experience. Her family, you know. Very big." He turned, catching Dalia's eye. "You might say she was raised in oil."

"Yes, yes," said Dalia. "From a little girl."

Grissom's forehead creased. " Chris? Tha's a funny name for someone from your part a th' world?"

Dalia shrugged. "Oh, it's just a nickname. You could never pronounce the one I was stuck with. I never use it."

"An' yuh speak so good?"

Dalia laughed again. "Well, like many upper-class young women, I was schooled in Europe and America. Lots of English from an early age."

Sydney did not like the direction of the conversation. "Well, we better get on." He checked his smart watch. "It's getting late. I think we have the idea, especially with those maps we have. Why don't we all go back and relax. Perhaps, Harv, you'd be so good as to answer some questions about the maps."

Grissom looked at Dalia. Her smile reflected promise.

Sydney's eyes sparked, momentarily. "You know, *tomorrow* we expect to see other facilities and where the water comes from and goes, and more. After all, we have big decisions to make, *right Chris?"*

Without waiting for her response, he started the vehicle.

***

Sydney's room was standard motel: queen bed, console with TV and restaurant guide, a mini-fridge beneath, a motel note pad and lamp.

They sat at a circular table near the window. Happy squeals could be heard from the pool outside. Sydney spread the plans before saying, "There are drinks back there at the bar, if anyone wants them. I'd like a Schweppes, Christi, if you don't mind."

Grissom extended a hotel glass. "Wouldn' mind a bit a gin, since ya offrin', kind sir." As he was the only one to accept, he made the most of the drink.

"Tha's the Pioneer operation," Grissom pointed at an aerial photo displayed between two ashtrays. "The biggest, but it's 'sentially the same equipment, just more a it."

Sydney traced the components with a motel pen. "Separator, tanks, well head. Got it."

"'Zactly," Grissom nodded, taking another sip. "Jes' more, like I said."

"Perfect," Sydney closed the file. "Can we explore water supplies tomorrow?"

"Sure thaing, just a buncha wells, but sure."

"And the reservoirs?"

Grissom's shaggy eyebrows furrowed. "Not where they git the frackin' water. Tha's for drinking. But ah'll show ya evathing. No botha 'tall."

Dalia, seated on the bed, smiled. "Thank you, Harv."

Grissom blushed in the light. "My pleasure, Chris. My pleasure, for sure."

Sydney stood. "Alright, it's been a long day. You could use some rest, Harv. So can we."

Grissom finished his drink. "Sure thing, boss man. What time is good?"

"Around ten. Work for you?"

"Ten it is. You're the boss." He headed out. "Goodnight, all."

Once the door shut, Sydney turned to Dalia. "What's with the flirtatious act?"

Al-Musawi glared at her. "Western education has spoiled her. I opposed using her."

Dalia faced him boldly. "Sure, one of your submissive flowers would fit, right? That your macho idea?"

Sydney intervened. "Kassim, she fits in here. But Dalia, tone it down. And you, Kassim, adjust. Don't complicate things further."

Dalia spun, her lips arched in a smirk. "American women flirt, so I am."

Sydney sighed. "She has a point, Kassim. Ease up. Dalia, don't push it. We don't know Grissom, or what he might do if he got ideas about you, my dear. Both of you, don't complicate this mission further."

Al-Musawi busied himself in the bathroom. Sydney motioned to Dalia. "Dinner in thirty?"

CHAPTER 12 WARNINGS AND FALLOUT

Big Pancho slapped his hand upon the dashboard. It reverberated with a *hum*. "So many fokking cars. Eet ees never going to end."

Panchito sought out the next sign. "Big Pancho, weel you shut the mouth? Callate! Why are we doing thees. Por que'?"

Big Pancho's sigh went on and on. His Pancho Villa mustache rose and fell. "Because we want to find thee Chevrolet."

"Si'". We want to find a sixteen-year-old Chevy in perfecto condition. Did we not go to the trouble of persuading that skinny gringo to tell us about thees Chevy?"

Big Pancho's mustache rose in a massive grin. "Si', we deed per— suade. Si'." He nodded his heavy head in satisfaction. "Persuade heem, new word?" The big Mexican studied his right hand. The knuckles flamed red. "Yes, per-suade."

Panchito glanced at his companion. *He ess strong but his memory is like, que' . . . maybe a retarded Chihuahua.* "Because . . ."

"Ahh, because we weel find about the putas that keel the Patro'n."

"That ees good, Beeg Pancho. That es muy bueno." A sign ahead said: Big Bart's One Thousand Percent Satisfaction Auto Corral.

Big Pancho craned his neck toward the windshield.

"What a fokking beeg sign."

"Si, beeg Pancho, an' look." Panchito gazed up at the car sitting upon a raised platform. A banner above proclaimed "Vintage Beauty. Collectable. Don't miss out."

Big Pancho's mustache furled and flapped. "Hey, Panchito."

"Si'. There eet ees. You gotta learn to be patient, Beeg Pancho."

"Si', pat—"

"Patient." Panchito turned into the lot.

***

With its modern buildings and snowcapped mountains, Tehran could be mistaken for many cities from a distance. But the Milad Tower, thrusting from its glorious pedestal and supporting a pure blue dome far above the tallest buildings, can only be found in Iran's capital.

In the House of Leadership, the Supreme Leader paced inside his office. "We hear nothing?" His piercing eyes focused on Minister of Foreign Affairs, Majid Abassi.

"No," said the heavy man whose neck was lost in several layers of soft flesh. "Nothing."

The little man with the black turban and a beard like Santa Clause sat down and rubbed his forehead. "Why did I trust this to the bumbling Lebanese hoodlums? Hezbollah. Paah! A bunch of ignorant peasants." He pointed a shaking finger at the other man. "Now we find out, because the bumblers in Beirut didn't think it was important, that the World Health Organization office in Beirut was robbed a month ago and the doctor's throat was slit. They say it was about drugs. But Hezbollah has been very quiet about the incident." His nerves were stirring too much for him to sit still and he began pacing before the faces of the mullahs once more. Framed in gold and close to life-size, the clerical portraits ranged along the walls. In silent agitation, Rouhani moved from one corner to the other as the Shiite religious leaders solemnly appeared to hold court under the pale yellow light of the expensive looking room.

"A strange risk to get drugs with heroine so prevalent," volunteered the other,

"unless . . ."

The little man in the black turban shuddered. "Hezbollah did it . . . and we put this operation in their hands. I am a fool for listening to you! You told me it would be sabotage—blowing things up—fire—not a medieval plague! What can come of this if the Americans discover?"

The Minister of Foreign Affairs thrust out fleshy palms from beneath his black robe. "The task was simple. Destroy their oil production for years. Did the Russians not sanction this? Did they not locate a man from the shadows who by reputation has never failed? Give this time. We do not know—"

The Ayatollah's fists pounded the air. "Do you think the Russians know? *Do you think the Saudis know?* They only contributed. Do you think if they thought it would be another Wuhan debacle that they would have paid a fortune—and put us in charge of it? *Do you, you imbecile?*"

"Nobody knew, Supreme Leader. How was I to know? Hezbollah does not trust us. They were to implement it so that neither we nor the Russians nor the Saudis would be directly involved. We weren't supposed to know the method or timing to avoid complicity. Those were the orders of the Guardian Council—" The minister's voice approached a plaintive pitch, immediately eclipsed by his superior's obvious exasperation.

"Do not shift the blame, Abassi," the Ayatollah screamed . His pinched face reddened around the white beard. *"This is your doing and you are the one who will pay if this turns into a disaster!"* The Iranian Supreme Leader quickly lowered his voice. "Germ warfare . . . We will be blamed, not those madmen occupying Lebanon. I do not care about the accursed Saudis, but what will Russia do?"

Abassi's heavy head contracted deeper into his neck. "Shall I alert them?"

The little man with the white beard could only stare. *"No, you abysmal fool! They will turn on us like rabid dogs. They will label us a pariah state. Aahh!"* In frustration, he yanked off his glasses. They bounded across the floor. The old man squinted at them dumbly. "We and we alone must stop this—if it is true."

The minister jumped at the opportunity to be of service. Mopping his glistening brow, he retrieved the glasses and handed them to Rouhani. "Yes. Yes, Supreme Leader, we could be making untrue assumptions." He thrust his substantial bulk up with effort. "All may be as planned. We do not know— in Allah's name, we cannot focus only on the worst outcome." His eyes registered the gravity of the situation as he braced for more disparaging rhetoric.

The tiny Ayatollah's dark pupils pilloried the man, literally forcing him back into his chair. *"Stop this insanity,"* he screamed. *"That is your primary responsibility, Minister. Your,"* he pointed a shaking finger, *"only responsibility. And if you fail, even Allah The Most Merciful will not save you!"*

***

Abu Ben Suliman leaned forward on a splendid chair of cushioned silk. In his rage, the Crown Prince's checkered ghutra spun erratically around his ears, as if a desert storm had penetrated the palace. To the small group of ministers in attendance, a storm would have been preferable.

Although younger than his advisers, the prince was ruthless. In his rise to power, he had banished many of his closest relatives. Some of the incarcerated had suffered worse penalties. His authority in Saudi Arabia was absolute and the General Intelligence Directorate, commonly known as the Mabahith, the secret police agency, enforced his decisions with ruthless efficiency. It was no wonder that the powerful men facing him were rigidly attentive.

There were five in attendance: First Deputy Prime Minister, Minister of Defense, Minister of Interior, Minister of Foreign Affairs and Minister of Justice. The King also served as Prime Minister. All remaining ministers, twenty or more were excluded from the meeting.

The prince breathed deeply to calm himself. His effort was only partially effective. "The Americans have been warned. If we are implicated, their rage will be like a storm that blows us away. Conservatives there have not forgiven us for flooding the market during the Trump Presidency. As you all recall, we tried to destroy U.S. fracking by glutting the market with oil during our staged 'dispute' with Russia, which was merely an excuse to lower oil prices below the fracking industry's level of profitability."

"Yes," gloated the Minister of Interior, a slight man of sickly pallor. "It was ingenious, was it not, Majesty? And now, their Liberals beg us for more oil, almost daily."

"True," nodded the prince. "With the heavy debt of those fracking start-ups, most went under. But the plan didn't fool that" — his eyes dimmed with long remembered rage — "Trump!" He exhaled past his full lips. "Praise Allah that that man was ousted and production diminished to levels of dependence upon us once again."

The skeletal Minister of Interior said, "But we must do something. This new president is 'America First' again, unlike his predecessor. What are we to do but work with the Russians again? It is about self-preservation."

The prince stroked his full black beard. He was given to smiling, but not today. "Of course. I know that we must stop their energy sources. With fracking, they produce more than all of us together, but," his pronounced nose swung toward each attendee in slow sequence, "the plan did not take into account a traitor."

Dark eyes widened, as members of the group surveyed one another furtively. He waved off their concerns with delicate fingers. The facets of his ruby ring exploded with red light. "Peace. I know it was none of your doing." His eyes narrowed. "It is a grave mistake that none of you would make. But someone in our ranks did. You know there are those of my family who still smart from their loss of power—would that I had killed them all. Now, because of this traitor, this Ya Ibn el Sharmouta, my accursed cousins know!" His darkly handsome face profoundly reddened as he slapped the arm of his chair. Reverberations rebounded off the great hall's golden ceiling. "And like the dogs they are, they alerted the Americans."

"No!" blurted out Faisal Al Sheikh.

"Yes, my dear Minister of Justice. They live in luxury in the delightful cities of the world and still seethe with jealousy. Now, we must contact the Russians and make sure that this does not rebound back upon us. Remember how the world treated China after their self-created epidemic. They lost billions. Their industries were moved back to the United States and Europe. They still haven't recovered."

"But that was a plague, Majesty," interjected Minister of Foreign Affairs.

"Yes, Hamad. And here comes another. Would the Americans retaliate if we are part of sabotaging an entire industry. . . perhaps causing many deaths in the process?"

"Yes, Majesty." The foreign minister was malformed, with hunched shoulders and a badly curved spine.

"You will alert the Russians through secret channels. We cannot be implicated any longer and, I presume, this would not be desirable for them either. The plan is no longer secret. It could be unraveled by their law enforcement, or CIA." His eyes became narrow slits. "I say again—and for the last time—alert the Russians. If they stay in, it is their business. But we want to be clean of this mess, if Allah grants us a way. Otherwise . . . "the prince fingered his beard.

"Yes, Majesty?" asked the minister.

The prince's wide-eyed smile bore no humor. "Why, we will need someone to blame, won't we?"

The five miserable ministers tensed visibly.

"It shall be done immediately." The deformed minister sat back down with some difficulty. His frightened eyes darted toward his companions.

All stared at their laps.

The Crown Prince sat a moment, then *clapped* his hands. All rose, hurrying off to their tasks.

As they hurriedly left the room, a man emerged from behind a ceiling-high tapestry depicting Muhammed the Warrior on Horseback. He wore a red beret and his camouflage shirt was adorned with red epithets above a chest full of medals.

"You've heard, Colonel?" spoke the prince. "Handle the traitor in my Council of Ministers. Ensure he survives long enough to divulge whom he communicated with among my chelb—" he cursed sharply. "Cousins, no matter the country or the international laws to be breached. Understood?"

The colonel saluted and stepped back. Disappearing behind the tapestry, he slipped into a concealed corridor leading out of the palace.

***

The frown Uri Karmov wore threatened to shatter the upper half of his face. He removed his hands from behind his neck, cutting short his daily isometrics. *The Americans know. The Saudi palace is a sieve. Who wouldn't know?* He flexed to release the creeping tension in his neck. *Do the Americans only know what . . . or do they know* how?

"What" is bad enough but "how"—pizdets! Fuck! Those insane Muslims! I agreed to sabotage, but what if it's worse? I was so busy, I never checked. Pizdets! I left this up to those bumbling Iranians . . . and those imbeciles left it in the hands of Hezbollah, a bunch of insane thugs.

He dug his palms into the sockets of his eyes until pain and colors appeared. *If something terrible happens, we must protect ourselves. Spanov obtained plans from someone in the States. That Texas Senator, I suppose? Can we be implicated? Do the Iranians know what the fuck is going on? Where is that phone?*

***

The Russian Embassy in Tehran is massive but with little imagination in its architecture. True, it does have lovely grounds within its high-fenced walls, but that just came with the territory. On the fifth floor, in a corner office overlooking the broad lawn, a Cultural Attaché'/GRU intelligence officer, Oleg Cassinov, replaced his phone. Daily sweeps assured the instrument's integrity.

His hands shook as he flipped out a Marlboro Vintage. *Damn things cost me a fortune but they are so much better than the shit here and I fucking need one.* He lit it with difficulty. *What have these Iranian shitheads done? What was their plan? We never should have left it up to them, but we wanted clean hands. Fucking sabotage—setting a fucking fire or blowing something up. How hard is that for these ragheads? Now the Kremlin is on my ass. They think the Council of Guardians has no idea what Hezbollah is doing. They are right. These morons fuck up everything.*

He pulled on the cigarette so deeply that it produced a

coughing fit. Smashing the costly Marlboro into a nearby ashtray, Cassinov took his head in his hands. *The Iranians hate Hezbollah and Hezbollah hates the Iranians . . . and I'm supposed to find out who Karmov's mystery man is. A man my own President didn't know.*

And even if I can—then if I have to find out what those maniacs in Beirut have put him up to. And the fucking Iranians aren't saying anything except that they paid the man a huge amount from all of the oil countries. I'll bet it was a damn fortune. But the bearded assholes didn't find out who they were paying. They said it was due to our recommendation and that it was our business. But it wasn't. It was left up to those maniacs in Iran. He reached for a second cigarette. *And the next day the account disappeared along with the money. No such account. Poof. Fucking millions!*

Cassinov took another puff. *How the fuck does that stonehearted bastard of a president expect me to find out?* His second cigarette was smashed into the first, tipping the cobalt ashtray.

Nothing else to do but go to Beirut. At the very least, they'll probably tear off my balls . . . those Muslims hate everybody. "Religion of Peace." My ass.

***

Kamran Fashi, of the elite Steadfast Commando Battalion of the Islamic Revolutionary Guard Corps in Iran, stood at attention before his colonel. His epaulette of three eight-pointed stars indicated First Lieutenant Fashi.

Although Iran had its share of military bases, this colonel worked out of a small cottage in a residential area.

It was set far back from the road. Behind gentle tulips and irises lining its walls, was state of the art security equipment, including lasers that could cut off an intruder's legs.

"Congratulations on your promotion, "said the colonel.

"I was fortunate, sir. There are many second lieutenants who could have—"

The colonel shook his head, waving him off. "No time for modesty. You are the best we've seen in a long time and you are going to prove that . . . immediately."

Fashi merely stood, knowing that the colonel intended to continue. The colonel, a fit man of fifty, reviewed a paper, although Fashi knew from his reputation that the officer had long ago memorized its contents. He looked up. "We have a problem of the first order, lieutenant. This is from the Supreme Council, itself." He awaited a reaction, but Fashi kept silent.

Pleased with his man's discipline, the colonel continued. "A member of the Russian Embassy, some attache'—who we all know is a cover for the GRU—has been inquiring about a top-secret operation out of Lebanon. Our sources in his embassy tell us that he plans to personally investigate. Knowledge of our involvement in this calamitous operation must be confined to the Council. It is imperative that this man never reach Beirut.

Despite himself, Fashi raised his dark eyebrows.

"Yes, I know, lieutenant. A Russian. But it cannot be helped. For him to succeed would cause the Supreme Leader embarrassment and worse. "Do you understand?"

After taking a deep breath, Fashi nodded.

"Good. Make sure that it is clearly an accident." The colonel tore off a second sheet, handing it to Fashi. "Here are his name and picture, and his routines when outside the embassy. Also places he frequents during his leisure time. Questions?"

He doesn't want any, Fashi decided. *He's already grabbing another file.* "No, sir." He saluted and spun crisply on his heels.

"By the way, lieutenant," the colonel stopped Fashi at the door. Without looking up he said, "You were previously deployed in the Corps of Microbiology and Virology, yes?"

"Yes, sir. Three years, before I transferred."

"From what I understand, the Council specifically recommended you because of your credentials. More than that I don't know. Good luck."

"Thank you, sir." Fashi wasn't sure that the engrossed man heard as he closed the door behind him.

CHAPTER 13 TROUBLE

Panchito and Big Pancho walked all around the car on the pedestal.

A tiny man in a big hat scurried toward them. "She's a beaut, isn't she. Just got her in."

They looked down at Bart. "Si', I like," said Panchito.

"A real classic," said Bart.

"Si', una classica," said Panchito.

Bart pointed at theirs, which was at least ten years newer. "You have a nice car over there."

"Si', pero me gusta esto." Panchito pointed at the Chevy.

The little man reached up a hand. "Howdy, I'm Bart, and I may be small but my deals are

he—uge!"

"Ah, si'," Panchito grinned. Turning to Big Pancho he said, "El senor es pequeno," he placed his palms close together, "pero sus negocios son . . ." his palms spread wide, ". . . grandes." Both men laughed uproariously.

The little man adjusted his monstrous 10 Gallon Hat to keep it from completely covering his eyes. *I got these greasers. They actually think that old line is funny.* "Come on into my office, boys and let's make a deal."

Panchito and Big Pancho trooped after Bart toward a shocking red mobile home. A slightly off-center sign above the door proclaimed, "Office Where Great Deals Are Made."

Bart retreated to a huge desk and sat. A stack of pillows

on his chair brought his head to six inches above the desk's surface. He lit a cigar. "Well, boys, how much do you want for your car?"

Panchito sat near the right side of the desk. "We wouldn't trade our car for that piece of shit, asshole."

Bart stared; mouth open.

"That's right, asshole. I speak good English."

Bart slithered deeper into the pillows. "Well, well, boys, I didn't mean to insult you. Not old Bart. Nossir." A wide grin bloomed under the shadow of his monstrous 10 Gallon. "So, you just want to buy the Chevy? That's great."

Unnoticed, Big Pancho had slipped behind Bart's chair. His huge hands quickly gripped the tiny man like a vice.

Helpless to squirm, Bart squealed, "I'll make you a great deal. The best, boys. No need for force. Bart'll take care of you."

Panchito ripped the cigar from Bart's mouth. "Hold his hand out, Big Pancho."

Despite his effort to resist, Bart's right hand moved inexorably down to the desk.

Panchito blew on the cigar. Its tip flowered glowing orange. "Who sold the car, Senor Bart?"

"I can't tell you." Bart's sales voice broke into a noticeably higher octave. "My transactions are privil— *ilege!*" His scream escalated as Panchito ground the cigar's bright end into the back of his hand.

Panchito shook his head. "Senor Bart, I do not like hurting you. Please do not make me do this thing again. All I ask is a little information. Por favor?" He blew at the cigar tip and the ash exploded with light.

Big Pancho flicked Bart's hat off with his elbow and pressed his shoulders even more tightly.

Teary eyed, Bart watched the pulsing orange ash descend. "No. I'll tell you! I'll tell you! I will!" His hand moved to a holster hanging near his right knee.

Panchito took a puff. "It is a very good cigar, Senor Bart. Go on, please."

After Bart finished, Panchito, still nursing the cigar, which was now a stub,

frowned . . . "And this car they traded for?"

Bart tried to wriggle his shoulders loose.

Panchito grinned, "Let him go. He is going to help, right?"

"Yeah. Yeah." Bart rubbed circulation back into his biceps. "Sure. Let me think."

Panchito's voice took on an edge. "Come on, Bart. You do not sell so many cars in a few days?"

Bart's large head bobbed rapidly. "Yeah. Yeah, it was a two-thousand-fourteen Honda. A Civic."

"And its condition?"

Bart's tiny forehead wrinkled. "Why great. All my cars are."

Panchito eyed his cigar butt. "Ba-art?"

"Looked great but . . . the engine leaked oil like a sieve. The shop I use patched it with sawdust and a clip, but any real pressure and it'll go."

"Like high speed on a freeway?"

Bart's tiny shoulders sagged. "Not even. Any road, doing over fifty for ten minutes." His eyes pleaded. Wincing with pain, he looked down at his hand. "Okay.

That's all I can tell you. That's it. Now I don't want any trouble—and this is just between us, boys—so why not let me get back to my business—"

"Sure, Senor Bart," said Panchito, "jus' one more thing. The license plate?"

Bart sighed, then reached for a small file box on his desk. His shaking hand knocked a Styrofoam cup to the floor. The little man stared as coffee slowly pooled onto the linoleum. He shook his head. "Shit." His tiny fingers dug into the box. "Uhh, here. Oklahoma plate. Here." He slid the dog-eared card toward Panchito.

"Thank you. Maybe we buy from you some day, Senor Bart."

"Yeah, yeah. Look boys, like I said, 'just between us', okay? I don't want any trouble."

Panchito's lips spread, revealing soiled teeth. "Sure, Senor Bart. Just between us." He looked up at Big Pancho, tilting his head slightly.

Already tense as a cat, Bart noticed. His hand groped the holster hanging near his right knee.

In the confines of the small office, the *crack* erupting from behind Bart was startling.

Bart's sprawled body was festooned with the colorful pillows from his chair.

"That was nice, Beeg Pancho. I don't think he felt a theeng. I liked the leettle guy."

"Me, too," agreed his companion.

They closed the door and walked toward their car. Passing the raised platform, Big Pancho smoothed his mustache and looked up. "That Chevy es un fokking bueno auto, no?"

"Si,' muy bueno," said Panchito, reaching for his keys.

***

Oleg Casinov sipped his coffee at the Baccara Café in Tehran. Strings of lights illuminated a two-story indoor courtyard. Reflections danced along the surface of a pool where the soothing tinkle of water from a central fountain lent itself to the peaceful motif of the surroundings. Potted red and white geraniums surrounded the pool, enhancing the relaxing ambiance.

He paid the check and left. *Wonder if there are any good restaurants in Beirut,* he thought. *Certainly not where those tight-ass Muslims control things.* He lit another of his expensive Marlboros and started walking.

The embassy car was parked on Edward Brown Street the next block over. Darkness was overtaking the city and the Russian was quite alone. Casinov ate by himself frequently because most of the agency personnel, in an effort to save money, or unwilling to try the local cuisine, preferred to dine where they worked.

All such conventional idiots, he often thought. *They live in a different country and won't venture out. Then they'll go home and lie about their time here.* The Russian laughed inwardly about the foibles of his countrymen as he prepared to unlock his car.

Headlights from behind froze him. *That is the first car I've seen,* he thought as he momentarily blinked into the glare. Waiting inside the half-open door of his car, he wondered, *That engine is awfully loud, right behind me—* The unknown car smashed into the door of his car, slamming it into Casinov. He flew into his car as if shot from a cannon. Portions of his face and head cracked open the moment he rammed into the steering wheel. His limp body gradually slithered back out and onto the street. The instrument of his death backed over his crumpled remains, then forward once more, before blazing off into the darkness.

During the following weeks, inquiries by the Russian Embassy were greeted with shrugs from Iranian officials. With no witnesses, what was there to be done about a hit-and-run?" A drunk from a café, no doubt. Eventually, the Russian investigators gave up. What else could they do?

***

Two days after the incident, Kamran Fashi stood before his colonel in Iran's capitol city. Neither spoke of the unsolved death of the Russian Cultural Attache'.

Again, the colonel took the time to review a document that Fashi knew was already clearly in his mind. "So, to review, you have extensive experience in matters biological?"

"Yes, sir," agreed the lieutenant, although the matter had already been discussed during their first meeting. "In 2020, I trained extensively in combatting the virus from China. Many of us were tasked with learning about such threats for the future."

The colonel nodded. He slid tickets across to Fashi. "You will fly commercial, not military, and you will dress as a civilian. Hezbollah does not tolerate oversight from us. Instead, you will be an expert on communicable diseases from the World Health Organization consulting with their regional office in Beirut. There is growing concern about Hezbollah activities among the Lebanese. They will validate your credentials and provide cover for you as an expert in infectious diseases and immunology. You may contact me any time by secure means. Here is my private number."

"And I am to find out?"

"Whether those Hezbollah maniacs have sent out a team to spread plague in the United States, specifically to oil producing areas. The W.H.O. regional office there will acquaint you with what was stolen from their facility there. The local doctor was killed and we believe Hezbollah is responsible. You are to find out."

After a pause, the colonel said, "The Council does not want this to go any further if biological weapons are involved. You are to do whatever is necessary to stop it. At *any cost*."

"Even an international incident?"

The colonel stared hard at his desk. "Yes, even that. But I pray that you can find a better way, lieutenant. We are all counting on you to do that, if at all possible. Use all of your considerable ingenuity to avoid such an option. You can well imagine the consequences that it might bring." The colonel stiffened in his chair. His eyes focused like lasers upon Fashi. *"Only as a last resort. Am I clear, lieutenant?"*

"Absolutely, sir. . . And if I discover that such weapons are not involved?"

For the first time the man behind the desk smiled. "If not, then, my dear lieutenant, it is the Americans' problem, not ours."

***

Sydney and the team spent their second day touring wastewater recycling facility that had been shut down for more than five years.

"This is the new thang," Grissom explained, as Sydney slowly weaved the car around clarifying tanks that opened up like giant craters in the earth. "Ain't no odor like reg'ar wells, if tha's what yore thinkin'. 'Cause it's mostly methane and that don' smell." He pointed at two towering tanks standing twenty-five feet high. "Them Separators git rid of the smelly stuff. Do a hell of a job, too. The city an' ever'one else been raisin' hell 'bout the regular water supply drying up—it's a freakin' desert here, ya know. So all these companies spent millions on recycling the used water from them wells on the site I showed yuh. An' everthing was fine. Then it all went ta shit when those idiots would'n let us do frackin'. Now, as frackin' kicks up, it's gonna be a scramble agin' an' these ol' boys like Concho Resources an' Waterbridge an' Midland Water gonna be spending lotsa' money all over agi'n on water pipelines and waste water disposal, caus'a them crazy Washington bastu'ds." Grissom leaned over from the back seat, so he was speaking close to Sydney in the front seat. His eyes narrowed as his voice dipped a little. "You take my word, we gotta git in good with those guys so we get priority." He winked at Sydney through wide rearview. "If'n yuh git my drift."

Sydney winked back at the mirror. "I'm sure we can make arrangements."

Satisfied, the Texan leaned back. He grinned at Dalia.

"Ah was shore ya'all could."

Dalia rewarded him with a soul-brightening smile.

After a late lunch, when they were back in the Mercedes, Sydney asked, "Now what about drinking water facilities?"

Grissom chugged his third beer, frowning. "Wha's thet got ta do with ana'thin'?

With his hand poised over the ignition button, Sydney turned to face Grissom. "Because, Mr. Grissom, we are *very thorough.* As I told you, we want to know *everything,* whether or not it makes sense to you."

Grissom's slightly dazed eyes focused fast. "Shore." He fluttered his palms toward Sydney. "Shore, whatever yuh say." His scraggly eyebrows bowed. "I know you the boss." He felt himself blush with embarrassment and shrugged at Dalia.

"Now drinkin' water is kinda tricky. Lot comes from wells fartha' away from the Colorado Rivah water shed or somethin' or otha." Although Grissom's heavy stubble was gone, presumably to impress, dark residue was growing back rapidly in its place. He stroked it with three fingers. "I got it. How's 'bout I show yuh our main treatment plant? You're gonna see how up ta date it all is. "

Sydney pulled out a cigarette, but didn't light up. "Sure, if that's where it all goes before it gets to us. That will prove it's safe?"

The Texan nodded his head vigorously. "Yessuh. Mos' all of it goes right outa there. Wait'll yuh see. Good ol' Midland's got a hell-of-a modern plant. It's bee-utiful."

Sydney lit up. "Okay, Mr. Grissom, we'll see that and

then," he opened his palms, "that ought to wrap things up. Which way do I go? "

"We'll take a right up at the end a' the block." Grissom's unkempt eyebrows arched. "Hope I'll be hearing from yuh."

"Absolutely," said Sydney. "You appear to be the man we need."

Grissom beamed at the group. "T-tha's great. Glad ta hear it. None a yuh gonna be sorry."

The trip to the facility was uneventful. They watched revolving arms spraying water above row upon row of tubs with monotonous consistency. After ten minutes, Sydney decided they had seen enough. "We'll drop you at your car," he told Grissom. "But be sure to give Chris your address and phone numbers—both home and cell."

"Sure. A course ah will. Chris . . ." Grissom rattled off the information as they drove. After he got out, he stuck his head back in. "Ah'll be waitin' by the phone. When yuh think—"

Sydney leaned toward the man, smiling. "Probably this evening with the time change . . . early tomorrow at the latest. Don't worry, Harv, getting you cleared is just a formality."

Grissom nodded. "Yeah, jus' a formality." He winked. "Ah know how thet goes." He backed off, waving. "I'll be waitin'."

Grissom kept waving as they drove off. "A damn long time, Harv," laughed Sydney.

"Damn long," echoed Dalia, laughing, as well.

***

Panchito dug into a taco smothered in green sauce. "Say, thees eesn't bad—not as good as home—but not bad." They had been together in their particular line of work a good many years now. And although Panchito's English was very good, Big Pancho's was not. Therefore, between the two of them it was always pidgin English, if not Spanish.

"Umph," replied Big Pancho through a mouthful of refried beans.

"So," Panchito gripped his earring, running a finger along its surface: a sign that he was thinking hard. "Eef their damn car ees such a dog, bleeding oil, what these guys gonna do weeth eet? By now they mus' know—"

The big man wiped the food dangling from his mustache. "No gonna get their dinero back, tha's for shore," He said it with a deadpan face and shrugged.

Panchito nearly spat out his gulp of Dos Equis. "Beeg Pancho, that ees very funny!"

"Oh, yeah?" Big Pancho chuckled. His eyes darted toward a fat enchilada. "So, they ain't gonna buy another auto to get aroun', si'?"

"No. They rent. Ees much cheap. An' where, if I was them—whatever these putas are doing—I'd wanna get my ass out when I'm done, rapido."

Crunching a guacamole laden chip, Big Pancho nodded. "Si', el aeropuerto," he mumbled without looking up.

Panchito *slapped* the table. "You got eet, Beeg Pancho. At thee airport. Finish, por favor. Thees ees the only thing I can theenk of. We look for thee Honda there, si'?" He tugged at his earring as he thought about the possibility, a sly curl forming at the corner of his mouth.

"Si', thee Honda," nodded Big Pancho and he pocketed the remaining tortillas.

***

After dropping off Grissom, Sydney and the team sought out food on the way back to their motel. It was early, but spending so much time with the Texan had made them all tired.

"If I had to hear that awful accent one more minute," Dalia said, "I'd pull all my hair out."

The skin around Sydney's eyes crinkled up. "I thought you liked him—a lot?"

The woman's green eyes flashed fire. "Like him? That fucking redneck? I was just trying to get more information—that's all. You *understand?*"

"Paah," Al-Musawi's thick lips twisted into a scowl. "You flirt. You flirt with anybody."

Dahlia had her neck craned to one side when she heard the big man talking. She slowly turned her head to the front and hissed at him. "We aren't in the Middle East, now, you arrogant barbarian. Keep it up and we'll see what you can do with a woman who isn't afraid of her own shadow."

Al-Musawi brought his face up to hers. His black eyes were two glowing coals. "Maybe we shall see—"

Dalia arched her spine as she hissed back at Al-Musawi. "Maybe we will."

"Will you two cut this bickering? *I'm sick of it!*" Sydney thrust the wheel so sharply that they all tipped left as the car hurtled right into a parking lot. *Family Style Dining* proclaimed the neon sign. They trooped into the diner in silence.

They were shown to a booth whose chintz curtains matched the table cloth's red and white squares. Once they had ordered, there was silence. Finally, Sydney puffed out a deep breath. "I will only say this once more. We need unity here. I can't work with amateurs who let nonsense get in the way of the mission." His blue eyes narrowed. "I won't. I have *never* failed and I won't let you two get in the way. Am I clear, *for the last time?*"

The man and the woman nodded without making eye contact.

"After we've eaten, we will get rid of this Mercedes. We don't need it and there's no sense in spending good money for it. Then we pick up the Civic. Remember, tomorrow, the serious work begins. I'll tell you the real plan, because I have to—not because I want to—the ridiculous way you two can act."

Their drive to Hertz was silent and without incident.

***

Midland International Air and Space Port is a rather grandiose name for a facility that is more provincial than anything. It has a humble looking food court, a news stand with a huge Texas flag dangling down, a typically curved ceiling above the check-in area and ample parking with many acres for future expansion. Of note was its FAA designation as a Space Center because it is the only commercial airport approved to offer orbital space flight by rocket planes, whenever feasible. Especially convenient, unlike some larger airports, the rental car desks and parking never required buses or trams. Everything was an easy walk. After checking into Hertz, Sydney and his team headed for the Civic. A late afternoon haze had settled over the concrete, draping the vehicles in a soft sheen. They had intentionally left their car at the far end of the lot, close to a lone water tower.

Al-Musawi was the first to catch sight of the massive glob of oil covering the concrete beneath the Honda. Prisms of color glimmered where the sun struck the oil. He slapped the Civic. "That little midget. I weel kill him! I weel crush his balls! I weel—"

"Enough!" yelled Sydney. "We can't go back. We can't afford to have an incident. Time is precious and this is an insignificant occurrence. We'll rent another car—not a Mercedes—and proceed tomorrow to the place I have in mind. One that will be a great surprise to anyone tracking us—although I doubt if anyone is. If all checks out, our time to execute the plan will be this weekend. Leave the weapons and extras here and we'll load them into our new rental."

***

Panchito peered past the crucifix hanging from his rearview mirror. "See, Beeg Pancho, they went right at thee Ceeveec, like I to'll you. "

"Right by thee Ceeveec, like leetle bees to thee hive." Big Pancho grinned. A huge gold tooth flashed. He reached beneath his seat pulling out a large revolver. Setting sunlight glinted from its polished barrel.

Panchito, in his long coat, stepped from the car. "We keep three rows away. Thee putas weel never see us until we wan' them to." He made sure the machete was in one deep pocket and also the Beretta Machine Pistol in his other. Testing its collapsible forward grip, the smaller man assured himself that it would instantly clear his inside pocket when he drew. He looked around, then at the distant terminal. He saw no one approaching. Their only company was a few scattered cars in the far lot. *Bueno.*

Big Pancho pulled his jacket over the revolver. "Eet gets cheely here by now, so no problema con los abrigos."

"No, no problem with thee beeg coats. Ees natural," agreed his companion.

"There ees la chica, Panchito. Jou see?"

"Yes, I see."

"Maybe eef shee ees pretty, no?"

"Si, eef she ees bonita, maybe no bullets for her until later, ay Beeg Pancho?"

Quietly giggling to themselves, they set off across the tarmac. A short distance from their prey, Panchito said, "Ees okay eef I do thee talking? That won' hurt yo're feelings? I would not want to do that."

Big Pancho gave his friend a hearty slap on the back. "No, Panchito, but eet ees muy bueno that you ask."

***

Dalia held the trunk open. "I need my sweater. It's cold."

"It's cold," mimicked Al-Musawi, but a glare from Sydney silenced him.

"Okay, but hurry." Sydney scooped up the plans they had used with Grissom. He cast them into the trunk. *Might still need these for the reconnoitering I have in mind between now and Saturday.* Sydney was just pulling his head back out from the car when a voice behind him said, "'S'cuse, senor, ees thees thee only place for thee coches?"

Sydney spun. Before him were two swarthy men in full coats, one small and one very large. Both smiled. "Wee cannot ver—see—our auto," said the smaller. With the fingers spread out, his hands looked large for a man his size. "Es muy grande," he laughed, shrugging his narrow shoulders.

Although Texas was an open carry state, Sydney insisted that they not carry weapons. He studied the men briefly, then relaxed. *Just some workers from around here, probably back from visiting the family in Mexico.*

Dalia watched from behind the open trunk as Sydney said, "Well, there *is* another lot over that way." Unconcerned, she resumed her search.

Al-Musawi advanced halfway around the car from the other side. He stopped behind the stooping Dalia, watching the two men closely. His left hand, hidden by her body, tapped her side insistently.

Panchito's dark eyes followed Sydney's pointing finger. Still smiling, he said "Ah, sí', sí'. Muchas gracias."

"Muchas gracias," echoed Big Pancho, following his friend until they were behind the two at the trunk. "Ah, sí'." He, too, pointed toward the other lot.

Musawi insistently prodded Dalia, signaling with his eyes at a Colt revolver that rested right next to her sweater. Uncertain why he wanted her to pass it, she slid the revolver to her bigger companion with a frown.

Panchito's machete flashed out, slicing Al-Musawi's arm as he raised the Colt. Both weapon and arm flew in opposite directions.

Al-Musawi roared in rage as bullets from Panchito's Beretta sprayed from his other pocket. With what sounded like "Allah," the Hezbollah fighter dropped, *splatting* into the pooled oil escaping from beneath the car.

Dalia scrunched herself further into the trunk. Grabbing a machine pistol, jammed against her face, she blindly released a cascade of bullets over her tightly squeezed body. The spurts mostly caught the dangling top of the trunk, but at least one burst perforated Panchito's waist. His machete *clattered* to the concrete as he stared, incredulous, at the red mush seeping through his raincoat. His top half flopped into the trunk, while the rest of him dangled downward. Only the toes of his small boots touched the ground.

Big Pancho bellowed, thrusting his revolver as he rushed toward the trunk. One burst of Dalia's random bullets had peppered his side, but all that he could feel was rage at what this puta had done to his amigo. He jabbed the gun into the trunk, intending to put one right between her eyes.

As she raised her arm, Big Pancho grabbed the 9 mm Parabellum from her hand, nearly snapping her finger inside the trigger guard. Before he could pull the trigger of his own weapon, the trunk's lid *thudded* down upon the big man's back. A harmless shot flashed from his Colt due to the immense force of the impact. Enraged, Big Pancho tried to twist around but the heavy lid descended again and again, crushing his windpipe and clavicle. Soon his legs were windmilling as his thrashing body slung half out of the trunk and his struggle for air became futile.

Still wedged inside the trunk, Dalia kicked at the dying Mexican's torso. On the way down, it dislodged his smaller partner's body. Both splashed into the spreading oil. Big Pancho stopped twitching as his and Panchito's blood reddened the already slick concrete.

Dalia slid from the trunk as Sydney lifted the lid. "Thanks."

"No problem," replied the tall man. Both looked down, trying to avoid the gory slime. Three tangled bodies lay entwined at their feet.

Tossing her weapon back into the trunk, Dalia wiped her eyes. Mascara mingled with perspiration, or maybe it was tears. "What do we do with them?" She avoided the mess as she stepped toward Al-Musawi. "I did not like Kassim . . . but still."

"I know," said Sydney. He paused a moment, locked in thought. *Didn't that bloody American politician say to never let a good crisis go to waste?* While Dalia leaned against the Civic, her free hand toyed anxiously with her hair.

Gingerly, Sydney grabbed Panchito's body under the arms. He slowly dragged it toward the driver's side. Yanking the door open, he sprawled the corpse onto the seat. Oil and blood quickly spread across the interior. Dalia rushed over. "The plans are getting—"

"I took them from the trunk and put them right where we need them," Sydney calmly informed her. "Right under his head. There's a little blood and gook on them, but they're plenty legible."

"But what if *we* need them?"

"Believe me, they are better here. And I'll let you know why soon. Now let's take our bags and only two weapons each. Leave the rest scattered in the trunk. Keep yours in your bag. I'll do the same. Hurry. There's just a little blood on you. We'll clean you up in the airport."

As they surveyed the scene, Sydney nodded. "Looks fine. Just one more thing." He removed a phone from his pocket.

"Isn't that the throw-away you used to call—"

"Very observant." Sydney smiled slyly. "This will be the finishing touch, I think." Walking back to the corpse in the car, Sydney wiped the instrument and carefully laid it on the plans near Panchito's head. Then he placed the dead Mexican's left hand over both. "That should do it. See if anyone's coming." Lights from the overhead poles closer to the airport were flashing on. None extended as far distant as the location of the Civic.

"No one," said Dalia. "I see some figures a bit closer, but not nearly this far."

Sydney reached for his soft-sided suitcase. "What say we rent ourselves a car?"

CHAPTER 14 DEEP THROAT GARAGE

Early sunlight flooded Flynn's corner office in the one-story building housing the Rangers in Midland. Stedmier studied Flynn's coffee ritual with amusement. "Yuh dunk that donut in yuh coffee one more time, Toby, it's gonna disintegrate right there in yuh cup. Then you'll be fishin' out the pieces for the next hour."

"Most productive thing ah done fur the las' two days, Sted," grumbled Flynn. "An' not a goddamn clue as ta what or where or *if* these fellahs ah even headin' our way. Mebbe that tip Artie got was jus' so much bullshit by a crazy A-rab. Sheet!" Without warning, the heavily soaked donut disintegrated into his coffee. "Sheet!"

Stedmier laughed so hard, a little of his coffee came close to sloshing into his own lap. "Tol' yuh."

Just as Flynn was about to respond, the same young ranger who had originally brought Stedmier to Flynn's office appeared at the door.

"Sir—"

Still fishing soggy crumbs from his coffee, Flynn looked up. "What ya got?"

"There's been a blood bath at the airport according to airport security, Sir. They need us right over there, *Sir.*"

Flynn practically jumped from his chair. "Well now, Davey. Jus' when yuh give up hope, the Big Man smiles down on yuh."

"From your mouth ta God's ear," said Stedmier, swigging down the rest of his coffee in a single gulp.

***

"I d-didn't t-touch anything, R-r-rangers." The young security cop stood respectfully to the side. From his deathly pale face, Stedmier and Flynn surmised that the traces of vomit floating on the pooled oil behind the car were his. "I came out to ch-check this far lot, c-c-cause usually there are no over-n-nights way out here."

Stedmier laid his arm on the young man's shoulder. "Ah un'nerstand this is tough, son. Just re-lax an' we'll ask what we need, okay?"

The youth's shoulders lost some of their tension. "I don't normally panic but—"

"Yeah, yeah, it's okay, sonny." Flynn knelt near the two bodies outside the Civic. "Jus' give us a few minutes. Then yuh kin tell us whatever's on your mind." He looked at the remains of the man with the Middle Eastern face. "Fucking arm's cut off," he yelled to Stedmier.

"No shit," Stedmier yelled back as he carefully handled the phone and plans in the front seat with gloved hands. "Hey, son, theh's a evidence bag in our car. You cain't miss it. Bring it, would'ya?" He thanked the young man as the bag was handed over. Careful to touch as little as possible of the two items, the Ranger dropped them into a plastic envelope nearly as large as an artist's portfolio. "Call the lab, Toby."

"Already did," replied Flynn and struggled to raise himself up. A spectacular *creak* disrupted the early morning quiet. Flynn's fleshy face erupted in red. "Damn knees ain't what they us'ta be, 'specially in the mornin'. Okay now, sonny, le's go over what yah got."

Now that his initial shock had passed, the young man's face regained its normal color. His chest rose up and out. "Yessir, just ask me anything . . . is it hard to become a ranger?"

Both Stedmier and Flynn smirked as the young hopeful strode proudly with them toward their car.

***

Stedmier, Flynn and Arthur Krause huddled at the conference table in Krause's office. After they cleared the table of Karuse's test papers and two thick engineering tomes, Stedmier trotted out the cellphone envelope. Lab found no prints on either a item."

"Let's see those plans," said Krause. He studied the bottom of a page with a large magnifying glass. "Good thing the blood didn't hit this, like those other sheets. Look at this, Dave." He slid the page to Stedmier.

The Ranger pointed the glass where Krause's finger rested. "Holy, shit. Well ah'll be—"

"A ring-tailed porcupine's left nut," added Flynn. "Nah git on with tellin' me what thet damn thing says."

"The U. S. Senate Office of Public Records," read Stedmier. "How the fuck? These are all about our oil fields here and over in Odessa—not jus' fracking but the whole shootin' match."

Taking back the glass, Krause peered again. "Maybe not, Ranger. See, I thought so." He pointed to a barely distinct circle.

Flynn bent over Krause. "Yeah. Looks like a wobbly pencil mark. You caught this? It's barely visible, Ahtie."

Krause shrugged but smiled. "Years of working with

maps. That's all."

"Sheet no." Stedmier slapped his friend's arm. "You the man!"

This time Flynn leaned over Stedmier's shoulder, squinting at the print. "Right by Pioneer's wells, looks like."

"Could be," said Krause. "My Arab friend was never that clear. I may have just assumed the threat was to a massive area."

"Well, this sure simplifies our problem. The Permian's a mightah big place, othawise." Flynn used Stedmier's shoulders to push himself upright. "I need a coffee. Anyone?"

"Nah," Stedmier removed the cell phone from the envelope. "Replaceable . . . but I don't think it's a 'Burner.' Hmm, tha's kinda sloppy."

Forgetting his coffee, Flynn walked back. "So we can trace calls on it? Hot damn."

Stedmier grinned. "We'll, we kin hope. An' there's only one number on it, which should make things easy."

"But to whom?" asked Krause. "The Arab or the ones who cut off his arm?"

Flynn said, "We're pretty sure the other two were cartel guys. Got some records coming in from Nuevo Laredo. But ah'll bet my bottom dollah tha's who they were."

Krause tilted his head toward the phone. "Then whose is this stuff, the Cartel's, or the others? They could have left too fast to remember it."

Stedmier frowned. "Don' seem like Cartels' business, does it? They don' mess with high visibility shit."

"Not since ol' Escobar blew up his own town back in Columbia," added Flynn. "An it ain't their type a play, anyway. They don' give a shit 'bout oil. Ah'm bettin' on the A-rab an' his pals."

Stedmier reached for the instrument. "Only one way ta find out, Toby. Let's git us a guy in ta check out the sim card an' run a internet trace. Should be easy." He frowned. "But ah sure don' get why it's not a dummy phone yuh cain't trace. Thought these cha'acters was too smart fuh that.

"Maybe they're not. Let's hope for small miracles," said Krause.

Stedmier snapped his fingers. "Hol' on. While our guys ah doing that, git someone over ta the cah rentals. How long ago ya think this all took place?"

"Yeah," said Flynn, "they musta rented anotha car, 'cause with the oil leakin' an' the bodies an' blood, they sure wasn't about tuh use that Honda. An it had ta be kinda late, 'cause the kid we saw had already stopped patrollin' fer the night, so he said."

"Le's git someone over ta the car rentals," said Stedmier. "Check all the folks rentin' from early as three, jus' ta play it safe."

"Got'cha," said Flynn.

***

The next morning, the man behind the desk with the many phones decided that it was time to move his tiny office. *That's my deal,* he thought. As a middleman, and with all the calls he handled, he didn't want to know too much about the people who contacted him. That's why he never stayed in one place for too long. He patted his ample stomach. In his business he relayed messages that could mean blowing up D.C., or buying eggs.

I don't know; I don't care, he thought. *And I keep moving, too.* He reached for his personal cellphone looking through his calls for the same furniture movers as last time, thinking they were good . . . and didn't ask questions.

Before the second ring, heavy pounding shook his door. "Texas Rangers—*open up now!*"

Fucking shit, he thought. *should've moved last week.*

***

Later, Flynn couldn't stop chuckling. "That bastard was mo' pissed 'bout someone using a traceable phone than how much time he may do. Kept sayin', 'ten years an' the fust time some asshole doesn't use a Burner.'"

Stedmier frowned out of his car window at the trees in front of South Loop 250, West. A hawk circled aimlessly in the wind above the gently swaying branches. "Tha's about all the guy knew, fer shit sakes. Some kinda clearin' house fer criminals. Doesn't know who pays him or who gets the damn messages. Jus' a middleman—he was fuckin' proud a' thet."

Flynn laughed. "Yeah, that ol' boy gonna be a middleman at Huntsville Pen'tentiary fer a good long time, less ah miss mah guess. At least he did tell us he's the one left them plans for Grissom. An' this Grissom's s'posed tuh be some drillin' expert, so mebbe Grissom's the link with these characters. Got my boys checkin' on where he lives. If he gits back later, they'll tell us. He leaves, they'll stop him. Either way, we'll see him taday. Mah guess is he's jus' a dupe an' don' know shit, but mebbe we get some descriptions from him." He stretched, then grunted as he got out of the Ranger vehicle. "God, this ol' body's gittin' tired."

Steadmier opened his door. "Your right. Mah guess, too. He's jus' anothuh dumbass but he musta seen 'em, ah hope. When we grab him, let's bring Ahtie. He's the expert. Mebbe he kin help us git more infamation outta' this Grissom character than we can by ourselves."

***

Grissom waited most of the night for the call. He was so full of hope that he woke up ridiculously early. Three horizontal bars across his answering machine's window meant he hadn't missed anything.

Too early for a few brews at Ernie's, he thought. *What the fuck do yuh do at five thirty in the mornin'? Ah know ah did a good job. Ah know they was impressed—jus' taking time ta clear thangs with the bosses. Tha's all. They'll be callin' soon an' then I can be a* man *again with a better job than evuh. Then my woman'll be back. Yeah, then she's gonna be back fo' sure.*

His cheek itched where the beard was growing. He rubbed at it tautly, frowning. *Gotta keep this thang unda control. Gonna have a big job soon. Gotta look th' part. Ah cain't sleep. Jus' gonna drive a while. Ain't seen a sunrise since ah got laid off—gonna be kinda nice. Like a new start.* He opened the door to his garage.

Sydney was about to open the door from the garage into the house when he heard Grissom approaching from the other side. Following his predatory instincts he quietly opened the rear door of Grissom's car, and silently crouched below window level. Holding the door ever so slightly ajar, he avoided the sound of its closing.

Grissom walked around his car, sat, and pressed the ignition. He always left his keys on the passenger seat when at home, so he never had to scramble around the house trying to find them. The motor *hummed* in the confined space as he fiddled with seat belt.

The Texan noticed an aroma. Cologne. Wrinkling his nose, he had begun to turn when a hammer-like blow slammed the base of his skull. He was unconscious even before his head cracked against the steering wheel. As Grissom sprawled half over the center console, Sydney checked all the windows. They were closed tight. Leaving the engine running, he exited the garage as he had entered.

Pre-dawn haze blanketed the streets. Vacant houses, indifferent to the gloom, sat silently on the rural route. No residents yet endeavored to begin their morning commute.

A block away, Sydney got back into his rental. It was a nondescript Chevy. Eye contact with his partner conveyed "mission accomplished." Ready at the wheel, Dalia gave it the gas.

***

A little after 11 a.m., Stedmier and Flynn rang Grissom's bell. "Not a bad neighborhood," observed the younger man.

"Yeah, he must'ave done pretty well before the closings," Flynn agreed as he jammed his thumb harder against the video bell. "Too bad about them empty houses. Some look in pretty bad shape. It must look like Dee-troit after General Motors dove inta bankruptcy. Damn." He rang a third time.

Both men stared at the door.

"The boys said he didn't come or go," said Flynn.

"I'll see if his cah's in the garage, Toby." Stedmier walked down a neat path of brick pavers bordered by the skeletons of dead decorative plants.

Playing with a thin pick to tackle the simple lock on the door into the garage, the ranger found that it opened with a turn of his wrist. Involuntarily, his head jerked back. Although there was no odor, instinct told him to cover his nose and leave the door open. The pungent, carbon monoxide filled air slapped his face and burned his eyes and nose. Between the stifling heat and the monotonous uninterrupted *drone* of Grissom's engine, Stedmier knew exactly what he'd find.

***

An hour later, with Grissom's body on the way to the coroner, Steadmier turned into the Midland office lot and killed the engine. "No damn leads, tha's for sure. Sheet, now ah know those Mex boys jus' got theh'selves inta more than they could handle. What did they need drillin' maps fer? Not a damn thaing."

Flynn shook his head. "Nah, wasn't them. Be suprised if those boys can read. Plans like what we found wasn' gonna do them no good. An' when we finally figured out where their car was . . . inside a coupl'a shirts, extra shotgun—not hardly good fer blowin' up wells." He snorted. "An' wouldn' yuh know, no serial numbers on the engine an' stolen plates. Big surprise, huh? They was cahtel all th' way, ah say."

Stedmier opened the office door, waving off one of the rookies who jumped to attention. "Yeah. We'll check their prints an' stuff, but that ain't gonna get us nowheh. Sheet, hidden way back there at the airport, all isolated, they mighta' jus' been out ta rob 'our guys, or anyone else who came along—but they sure wasn't our saboteurs. Ah'tie, yuh got a take on this?"

Krause, who had followed them in, thought for a moment. "You know," Krause's eyelids dropped in concentration, "this Grissom certainly knew his stuff from what I hear. They must have asked him a ton of questions, a lot about fracking—if that circle on the map is any guide. Not so much about regular drilling sites."

Stedmier said, "Yeah, tha's sure. So, they gonna hit one or more a th' frackin' operations, yuh think? Pioneer's the biggest."

"Yeah, Pioneer," agreed Flynn. "Sure could be."

Krause stared out the window of Flynn's office. Traffic along 240 South Loop was picking up as the evening commute began. He chewed on his thick bottom lip. "You know, there's only one thing that bothers me . . ."

Flynn whipped around, staring at the little man, as did Steadmier. "Well, what, Ahtie. C'mon. Spit it out, man!"

Arthur Krause stared at the rangers, but his eyes were focused inward. "After two days of studying all that fracking equipment and well locations, which they must have done with that poor man, Grissom, why didn't that circle include water sources? There's miles of pipes bringing in water from other places, because they can't use city water. And why not recycling plants? If you want to destroy fracking, you might as well cripple their water supply, too. Otherwise, it's too easy to diagonally drill other wells."

Stedmier slapped his thigh. "Tha's a point. An' hey, we also gotta find out how they got the plans. Did they steal 'em or did some fuckin' senator give 'em to a bunch a' terrorists. With the A-rabs involved, that's what I'm thinkin'. We got ourselves damn terrorists."

"Terrorists, fuh sure," echoed Flynn. "We bettuh git the boss to contact Interpol an' find out 'bout ragheads on the loose."

Krause chewed on his lips "Would be a good idea to check around the sites. They're all getting set up and I know most a the foremen. A lot of them must have known Grissom over all his years working there. Maybe they can ask their crews if anyone saw him on the sites."

Stedmier snapped his fingers. "Sure . . . someone had tuh of seen him and whoevah' he was with. If we're lucky, mebbe we git some descriptions for our forensic boys tuh sketch up."

Flynn said, "Hell, yeah. Mebbe with a little luck we startin' ta untangle this here mess. But, damn. There shore are a shitload a' possibilities."

"I'll say. Terrorists, senators, and cartels." Krause shook his head. "As you Texans say, 'You sho' got'ya work cut out fer yuh, don't you?"

Wrapping his arm around the little man's shoulders, Stedmier said, "Not a bad accent for a amateur. Don' think you getting' outta this so fast, professor'. You done been drafted by *the Texas Ranguhs.*" Stedmier pointed toward the framed certifications hanging on Flynn's wall.

The three got up, laughing. As it went with law enforcement, Grissom's death soon became another forgotten piece in a much larger puzzle.

CHAPTER 15 MEANWHILE IN ANOTHER GARAGE...

Lieutenant Fashi , using his manufactured credentials, was greeted with polite contempt by the new doctor at the World Health Organization in Beirut. In truth, Lebanese Christians, like the doctor, had little regard for the Shia fanatics after the fall of the Shah.

"Yes, it was very tragic and shocking losing a dedicated doctor that way, Doctor Fashi," said the small man with the neat goatee. "So you are an immunologist and—may I add—very highly regarded according to the Iranian government."

"You honor me, Doctor Hariri. I fear they have overstated my expertise."

"You are too modest. But, be that as it may, how may I help you?"

"Let me be frank, Doctor. During the unfortunate incident here, we understand that items may have been stolen, as is often the case with such a crime. Criminals breaking in for drugs—"

"Yes, that was certainly the case," Hariri nodded his head while tsk, tsk-ing. "Doctor Zaud stayed late and must have tried to stop them, poor man."

"Yes, Doctor?" prompted Fashi. "Did anyone do an inventory?"

Hariri's back stiffened. "Of course, it is standard procedure, is it not? It was done as soon as I could get things settled here."

Fashi smiled at the pompous man. "Of course, Doctor. I never doubted—"

Still piqued, Hariri rushed on. "We have a complete list." He rose, moving toward a high file cabinet.

"No need, Doctor. We are especially interested in any biological cultures. That is why I was sent. To determine if anything stolen could cause major health problems. Drugs and pharmaceuticals are not at issue."

Hariri's small face compressed around his large nose. His back arched. "We do not conduct such experiments here. You should know that. This is not a laboratory or research facility!"

The lieutenant raised delicate fingers. "Please, Doctor. No one is accusing anyone and certainly not someone new like yourself. But I must inquire."

Hariri looked at his watch, sighing, "Doctor, I must be off to a very important meeting." He ripped open the cabinet's top drawer, jabbing his fingers into a row of files, retrieving a thin one and holding it out to Fashi. "Here it is. Please be my guest. I will see you later."

After the doctor's hurried exit, Fashi sat down at the man's desk, studying the neatly typed list. It wasn't long before something caught his eye. Hurriedly, the young lieutenant replaced the file and left.

***

Trying to overcome the grogginess of a sleepless night, Stedmier drank three cups of Flynn's black coffee.

"Yuh still look like a damn zombie, Sted. If'n my coffee don't keerect that, nothin' will."

"Can't help it, Toby, somethin's not right here." He

jabbed a finger at one of the sheets spread upon Flynn's conference table. "Is a goddamn U.S. senator involved? Ah hate tuh believe it, but how in God's name do these show up in a damn terrorist's car? No fuckin' way, 'less'n he or his staff got these over tuh that middleman to deliver."

Flynn nodded. "Yeah, but that middleman said it was Fed Ex'd an' we checked the return address he gave us. No such place—a damn dead end. Some

D.C. pharmacy that didn't have a clue. Although . . . D.C.?"

"Yeah, tha's somethin'. An' Congress was in session . . ."

Flynn's palm slapped the table. "And what would some dumbass sen'tor's staffer think ta do but send it FedEx, which anyone can trace. Damn it, Davey, we need more hawse power on this. Why don' yuh call headquartuhs?"

Stedmier puffed air through a chink between his lips. "Guess you right. If'n those Washington cha'cters are involved, it's way above yours an' mah pay grade."

"Hey, one sec," said Flynn, as Stedmier reached for the phone. "The boys came up with the results from them cah rentals. From three ta closing, twenty- seven wen' out, ten from Hertz. Six already turned in, so they prob'ly ain't the ones, 'cause these terr'ists would still need wheels. Got two guys workin' on contacting' the other customers. First eight checked out okay. I'll keep yuh posted."

"You do that. Mah guess is it'll be the one with phony info on their contract. Lemme know when that shows up an' at least we'll get a description on the vehicle." He reached for the phone a second time. "Now le'mme make this call, will yuh?"

***

Spanov's phone had been answered twelve times since early morning. Each time the reply to the staffer calling from Arlo Grossman's office was the same: "Attaché Spanov is not in the building. No, we do not know where he is. Yes, I will take a message."

Every time that Arlo Grossman's aide repeated the same information, Grossman's already troublesome blood pressure elevated. The senator, sitting in a medium sized office in the Russell Building, kept on squeezing a mushy ball in his palm. If it was meant to alleviate stress, it wasn't doing its job.

Being too distraught to eat a full lunch at his favorite restaurant, the Charlie Palmer Steakhouse, Grossman ordered from the Russell Carry-Out downstairs. An aid brought his soup and sandwich before he was shooed away by the nervous senator.

Grossman removed his thin glasses and polished them feverishly for the sixth time in an hour as he wondered, *Where is Spanov? How could that bastard leave the words "Senate" on the plans he sent—to whomever the hell he sent them? It had to be on purpose. Have I been set up— part of a Russian scheme? My God, what if the FBI is called in?*

Heat enveloped his head and neck, although the air-conditioning was working full blast and the window was dimmed with inside frost. *What if the sabotage kills people? What if the fires spread to homes? Oh, God, I'm going to be sick.* Grossman tugged in his considerable stomach and vomited into his waste basket--and vomited again. Soon there was nothing left. He sat there, miserable, drenched in perspiration.

At 5 p.m., the aide stuck his head in. "Anything I can do before I go, Senator?"

"No . . . thanks." Grossman quickly waved a goodbye and the bright young face disappeared behind the closing office door. "Have a nice evening, Senator Grossman. See you in the morn—" The voice was cut short as the senator closed his door.

Grossman stared around his office: honorary plaques; framed newspaper articles—photos of himself smiling with an array of notables with civic awards. His smiling face with mothers, religious leaders, local mayors and union leaders. Always smiling. *Where is that smile now?* He walked toward a mirror near the door. *Haggard. God, you look ten years older. Got to call Mimi.*

Grossman wandered back to his desk, plopping down into his swivel chair. It *creaked. Yeah, I'm fat. Got to admit it.* His wife answered on the second ring. Her voice was worried. "Thought you were going to be early tonight, Arl. Anything wrong?"

The sound of her voice washed through his soul. *God, do I love her. Best thing ever in my life, even counting the kids.* Grossman sucked in his gut and sat taller. "No dear, just a little extra work. I may be tied up a few hours. Sorry . . . you know I love you."

"I love you too . . . are you sure you're all right? None of that arrhythmia you had last year?"

"No, no, dear. It's all holding up fine. And starting

now, I promise I'll lose some weight."

"Oh, that's a good idea." She played along as if she hadn't heard his resolution a hundred times before.

"So, I'll see you in a few hours, okay?"

"Okay, Arl, my dear. Dinner will be take-out then?"

"That's fine. Bye." He lowered the phone. *How will I tell her, or the kids? If this thing blows up in my face.* His hands spread on the desk and he leaned his head between them.

A tune from *Fiddler on the Roof* awakened him. He grabbed for his cellphone. "Yes?" Relief spread through Grossman's chest. It was Spanov.

"I understand you have been calling?" The Russian's voice was calm.

Grossman thought, *I can't believe he sounds so composed.* "Calling? Yes, calling and calling. Where have you been?"

"Not your concern. Why have you been bothering my staff?"

"Why, *why?*" Grossman's normally high voice went falsetto. "They know. You sent the plans with the Senate marking. How could you people be so stupid!"

"Calmly, Senator, calmly." Spanov's customarily harsh voice quieted as Grossman's rose. "An oversight by my staff. There are simple solutions. My team has contingency plans, I assure you. You have nothing to worry about."

The steel bands constricting Grossman's chest slowly relaxed.

"Good. Thank God. How?"

"There are always ways, Senator Grossman. It is easy,

but I cannot talk about that on the phone."

Grossman drew in a deep breath. "Please tell me. I can't go on like this." Hope warmed his tense eye sockets. "Please tell me—I must know."

There was a *sigh* on the other end. "Very well . . . where is your car parked?"

"Hall of States Garage . . . 400 North Capitol—"

"I know where it is. It is open till ten, I believe. Meet me there on floor four in forty-five minutes."

Grossman clutched the phone so tightly that his wrist ached. "I will. I will. Great. Thank you, Mr.—"

"Actually, Colonel," came the reply. "Do not worry, Senator. And don't tell anyone about this."

"Of course, not—you think I'm crazy? Goodbye," Grossman said, but the line was already dead.

***

The streets around government buildings in D.C. vacate rapidly after 5:00 p.m. In the silence, Grossman's footsteps sounded louder than he could ever recall them doing. Litter from the day, illuminated by strong streetlights, sprinkled the curbs. It was lonely under the darkening metal sky, but after the hours of tension, his mood was the best it had been all day.

No one greeted him. Only the automated ticket machine was on guard. Grossman frowned in the elevator. Did he smell urine? He stopped at the third floor and entered his car. It was the only one left. He turned up the ramp instead of down. As he pulled onto the 4th floor, headlights flashed a hundred feet away. Only one other car was visible in the dimness. He accelerated toward the lights.

***

By 10 a.m. the news of Grossman's death was everywhere. *Senator's Suicide* read one headline. *A gunshot to Senator's temple,* came from another more imaginative tabloid. Rumors about an FBI investigation, of missing Senate documents and investigation by the Texas Rangers were rampant by the late edition. That night, Mimi and the family fled the city for her father's ranch in New Braunfels, Texas.

***

Colonel Uri Spanov watched the clouds enshrouding his Aeroflot jet. *Soon we will be above,* he thought. *A shame, this sudden departure, but things in the States may soon be sticky and the president wants me out—for good.*

Ordering vodka was very unusual for the fit colonel, but he decided that he deserved at least one. Flipping his recliner seat back, Spanov mentally reviewed his phone call with Karmov.

The president had sounded more relaxed than during their previous conversations— "Excellent, Uri Ivanovic. You leaving the identity of the Senate on the plans will cause turmoil in America when whatever happens, happens, but—" Karmov's ominous laugh had reverberated in Spanov's ear—"you will be nowhere to be found."

The conversation played back verbatim in the colonel's head. "But, Mr. President," he'd said, "I was careful, as always. No one could tie me in—"

"No matter," Karmov retorted with his usual arrogance. "This is the safest way."

Spanov snorted in his aisle seat, letting the vodka

permeate his awareness. *What could I say but "Yes, Mr. President?"*

"And," Karmov continued, without regard for his subordinate's feelings, "this Senator's death will be another American crisis— a pro-oil fanatical circus of Republicans versus anti-oil Democrats and their joke of a press. And amidst all the chaos, our government is in no way involved. Goodbye."

As Karmov had broken off, Spanov could have sworn that his President was laughing. The colonel's fists clenched. *Even with all that I have done, that bastard pulls me from the cushiest post that I have ever had. And for no reason! Fuck Karmov and his, "Whatever happens, happens. I'll probably get one of those miserable countries that end with "stan" for my next assignment.* He sought out the steward. *Fuck. I need another vodka— and this one, a double.*

***

For the third time in a week, First Lieutenant Mohammed Fashi stood at attention. Once again he was struck by the contrast between the cottage's flowery exterior and the brutally stark interior of his superior's office. It consisted of a metal desk with a glaring table lamp, a filing cabinet with one overflowing drawer jutting out, a single folding chair and a surprisingly empty wastepaper basket.

The colonel shook his thickly bearded head, after reading Fashi's report. For a long moment, his superior just stared, jaw muscles tensing. Then he uttered a deep sigh. "This is as the Council feared—just as they feared. Those insane fanatics . . ." His commentary was directed more at himself than at Fashi. The colonel picked up his phone, mumbling too low for Fashi to hear. Suddenly, he *crashed* it down. "You, lieutenant, wait here. No time to talk, and I must be off to the House of Leadership. *Now!*"

*** ***

If the House of Leadership wasn't surrounded by extensive grounds, nearby pedestrians might have heard the explosion from the Supreme Leader's office. His rants continued for over five minutes. Once done, he dropped down in a large chair that dwarfed him, breathing deeply.

After gathering strength, the Supreme leader commenced cursing a second time, half silently and half aloud. Finally, he sat perfectly still, willing away the turmoil from his mind. When sufficient calm returned, he opened his door and summoned an aide. The young man's nervous demeanor indicated that the Supreme Leader's rage had not gone unnoticed by those outside his office. "Send for Colonel Shadan."

When Shadan was ushered in, he inquired as to the Supreme Leader's health. In response, the selection of epithets regarding Hezbollah might have shocked even the hardened veteran. Embarrassed, the colonel bowed his head for the duration.

Once the rant ended, the Ayatollah politely thanked him; called him "brother" and "patriot", and remembered him to "Allah the Merciful." Then he motioned his visitor toward a chair. "Please sit."

Summoning the same terrified aide, the Ayatollah ordered tea. Almost immediately, the youth returned with a shining copper samovar. After pouring its contents into two narrow-waisted glasses whose sides steamed up immediately, the youth bowed and left.

The Supreme Leader gingerly gripped the hot glass. "Have some, please, Colonel. As he did, his diminutive host savored a taste. "Ah, Persian tea . . . it sets the nerves at rest, don't you agree?"

Even with tension streaming throughout his slightly shivering limbs, the colonel replied, "Yes, Supreme Leader. You honor me by sharing."

"Nonsense, Colonel, it is you who have done our country and God a great service . . . and now I must ask another."

The colonel replaced his glass. "Anything, Supreme Leader."

"Is that man, a lieutenant, I believe—"

"First lieutenant" blurted the colonel, automatically. His face, beneath the beard went crimson. "My apologies—"

"Peace," said the Ayatollah, waving it off. "Is he capable of a very important mission? *Very* important.

Nodding solemnly the colonel said, "Yes, Supreme Leader."

The man with the ragged beard thought for a moment, and then his dark eyes narrowed. "Then here is the special mission I have for your loyal Steadfast Commando Battalion."

***

"Are you ready for more travel, Fashi?" From Colonel Shadan's tone, the first lieutenant gathered that the question was purely rhetorical.

"Yes, sir."

"Ultimately to America?"

Only with great effort did Fashi control his surprise. "Yes, sir."

"Your English is excellent."

"Many relatives returned after the Shah, sir. I learned from an early age."

"You will receive a temporary study permit from the Embassy of Canada in Turkey. We already downloaded your application and it should arrive later today. It is very easy to cross over the border there—none of the problems like Mexico. You will stay in Ottawa at the address on your envelope. Once there, local Iranians living there will guide you through everything."

"Yes, sir. What shall I be doing?"

Shadan slid over a large envelope. "These are pictures of two of the Hezbollah team. These were obtained only by threat to withdraw military and financial support for their future operations. Even then, I understand there was a fierce internal battle before Hezbollah finally released them."

Fashi reached for the envelope.

"Their third is unknown. South African, I believe, but no one has a picture. Amazingly, not even the Russians. They usually have dossiers on everyone—even each other." He sat back. "Very strange. Whoever he is, he is a very skilled and unusual man. Keep that in mind, lieutenant. Keep it very much in the forefront of your mind."

"I will, sir."

"We are reasonably certain that the target is most

probably in Midland Texas. The oil fields are there." He sighed. "If that were truly the case alone, we wouldn't care at all."

"Then what is the problem, sir?"

"It seems those Hezbollah fools may have initiated the virus which was stolen in Lebanon."

"God!" The word escaped from Fashi's lips before he could restrain himself. "That is what the files I read were about."

Shadan's eyes clouded. "Exactly, lieutenant. Just as we feared. It cannot be allowed." He stared at nothing in particular, then gripped his trimly bearded chin. "I don't care if a million Americans die, but biological warfare . . . where can that lead?" The colonel's normally stoic face reflected concern that even the lieutenant couldn't dismiss. He stood up and began pacing the room.

Fashi had never known the man to show a moment's weakness. Nor, during all the time of their relationship, had Fashi ever experienced a moment of closeness with the colonel. Neither had his youthful companion officers. In their eyes, the man was a rock. Although this revelation was deeply disturbing, the lieutenant's face remained impassive.

Shadan's eyes refocused. "To whomever you reveal this information is entirely up to you. But it must be with only those qualified to stop the entire operation—*and discreetly, above all.* We are not looking for a public relations coup. What the Americans think of us is absolutely of no consequence, so make sure that you share this with the fewest possible. And *on the condition of absolute secrecy, now—and forever.*"

"Yes, sir. Understood."

"And the Battalion will forgive you, but regrettably, you must shave off your beard completely."

Again, Fashi fought down emotions. This time it was even harder. His beard was his pledge to God.

Apparently the colonel was gratified by Fashi's stoicism. Shadan's nod acknowledged admiration. "May Allah the Merciful guide your steps. Our Supreme Leader has chosen you for this task. Do him honor."

Fashi fought hard to manage an even tone, "Thank you, sir, I will," he said through a trembling throat and with a palpitating heart.

CHAPTER 16 PLANS, COUNTER-PLANS, AND BACK-STORIES

In the Supreme Leader's office, the mood was tense. Only Abassi and a translator were in attendance. The tiny Ayatollah stared out at the panorama of trees whose leaves sparkled in the sunlight. *How nice to be one of those little birds darting twig to twig right now. Look at them. What do they know of the trials men go through?*

Composing himself, he reached for a very special phone. It was gold in color and constantly monitored for extreme secrecy. It also had a scrambler for special calls. On this occasion the call was to his embassy in Moscow. From there, a second scrambling device would relay him to the Kremlin. Karmov, unwilling to use languages other than his own—some said he wasn't bright enough to master them—would also have an interpreter at his side. With a deep sigh, the Supreme Leader nervously awaited the connection.

***

The President of Russia grabbed a lozenge. His throat was raw from screaming into his phone for the past twenty minutes. His interpreter, a bespectacled young blond in his twenties, remained entirely impassive as Karmov hurled emotion-charged epithets at his Iranian counterpart.

Karmov's fists clenched. *Oh, if I had only had him here . . . I would have wiped his ass with that ridiculous beard of his.* The thought amused him, although his pale blue eyes failed to reflect it. Again, his powerful fingers spread, clawlike. *Oh, if I could twist that skinny neck.* He pressed his hands together, applying forearm isometrics to dissipate his rage. Finally, his anger slightly subsided. Thinking about his dressing down of the cleric, Karmov smiled to himself. *The threats of cutting them off from weapons and aid; competing with their oil; cracking down on Muslims in Chechnya and Tatarstan; withdrawing support for their thugs in Iraq and Syria— these would all be very effective, would they not? Could I . . . or would I do it all? Probably not. But the point was, bluff or not: clean up this insane biological insanity or I will stop supporting you.*

He stared through one of the high windows, wondering how long the fair weather would hold. *Those savages are nothing without us. Them and their stupid little boats against aircraft carriers. Hah. Such self-important little men. "Useful idiots," I believe the Americans say.*

The fit man with the balding crown leaned back. *At least we are out of it. Spanov is back at headquarters pushing papers and his senator friend is dead. Iran wouldn't dare implicate us. And the Saudis—fuck them. They turned their back on our mutual agreements to overproduce back in 2019 to destroy fracking. Their sweetheart deals with the Americans were much too valuable for them to cooperate for long. He shook his head. Why worry about them? Between their American lobbyists and the Prince's secret police, the Teflon Saudis will never get blamed.*

No longer concerned, Karmov turned to other business.

***

Stedmier was fiddling with pancakes at the Waffle

House. "Damn, ah always pour on too much syrup."

"Thet should be our biggest problem," Flynn said, staring at the crumbled donut pieces floating in his coffee. "Good thang Ahtie found thet fine printin' on the plans . . . jus' looked like nothin' tuh me."

"Me too, Toby. Pretty embarrasin' getting' out-sleuthed by an oil nerd." He took a bite of the pancake. "Ehh, this thing is soaked!"

Flynn smirked, his full pink cheeks rising to just under his eyes. "Yuh do it ever' time."

"Yeah," agreed Stedmier, watching syrup from the piece on his fork drip steadily back toward his plate. "An lookit them floatin' donuts a yours."

Flynn's grin disappeared. "Seriously, Sted, thet circle eliminated a whole lot a land."

The younger ranger pushed aside his plate. "Well, Pioneer Resources was always the best bet but, Jeez, thet's a lotta territory an' a shitload a' equipment on those other spreads we just e-liminated with ol' Ahtie's circle."

Flynn wiggled his bulk to free himself from the booth. "Well, might as well git at it. Why don' we call the oil nerd. He may have some ideas 'bout where tuh begin."

"Yeah," said Stedmier, grabbing the check. "We bettah have a plan a'fore we panic those ol' boys at Pioneer. They got enough on their plates starting up after all this time."

"They good ol' boys, fer sure, Sted. They'll do wha's right—an' I got the check." Flynn grabbed it from Stedmier, handing it to the smiling cashier before his friend could argue.

***

Sydney and Dalia had a quiet dinner near the motel. They had managed to find a little Italian restaurant. Wine bottles wound in rope and draped in candle wax provided flickering relief from the harsh lights of the commercial district.

The tall man held his glass to the light. "Not too murky." He sipped. "I am surprised. This really is quite good, considering." He tipped his glass toward her. "Here's to the mission."

Candlelight danced in Dalia's large black pupils. Her hair was worn long and flowing for the first time and touches of light eye shadow made her irises fathomless lakes in the dim lighting. She sipped, caressing the glass with full lips. Her eyes focused on Sydney. She said nothing.

Sydney's breath caught for a moment. *My God, this woman is beautiful. The business leaves so little time to notice—but now . . . We have four days to the weekend and nothing to do.*

Her eyes told it all. Sydney was not unaware of women's signals. He didn't need to feel her toes crawling up his leg to know she was feeling the same as he was. "I'm not very hungry," he said. "Maybe just a little more of this wine?"

"Yes, just a little more," she said. "Can't have a good bottle go to waste. Can we?"

***

In his room, Sydney left the bathroom door slightly open. It cast just enough light to give their bodies an air-brushed effect as they undressed. Hers was flawless, anyway, but the low light tended to soften the scars across his chest as well as the jagged veins riding his biceps.

They sat on the side of the bed, drinking in what they saw. Then the passion could not be resisted any longer and each began touching, fondling and kissing the other with gasps of longing. She was already wet as Sydney gently penetrated. As her *moans* of mindless ecstasy drove him on, Sydney thrust deeper and faster until both were uttering the gibberish of extreme rapture. He prolonged it by gently flicking his tongue inside her ear as he worked his way around, discovering her most sensitive areas. He made sure to linger at each one until she softly convulsed. Both of them arched as they gave themselves over to total release simultaneously.

***

Later he smoked, studying the white wisps gyrating gently in the cool currents from the vent above. Her head nestled in the crook of his arm. "Tell me about you—whatever you can."

He debated a moment, then released a jet of smoke and crushed his cigarette in his palm. "No smoking room," observed Sydney. He laid the butt on a night table. "I'll flush it later." Expelling a huge breath, Sydney made up his mind. "Okay. Well, I grew up on a lovely farm in Orania in the Northern Cape of South Africa. Normal life, good food, large family, much work, and closeness like most never feel in urban societies."

"What about the blacks?"

"As a kid, I didn't know or care. Didn't affect me. We had no slaves—didn't even know what they were till . . .

later. Yes, years later." His voice lowered to a level she could barely hear. "By then I was eleven, starting to think of girls and what I wanted to be. It wasn't going to be the farm, that was certain." His eyes narrowed to slits. "Well, that decision was taken right out of my hands, wasn't it?"

At his change in tone, Dalia propped herself up on one elbow. Tendons flared along his jaw as his eyes clouded with distant memories.

"I said I hadn't even seen a black except on rare occasions. Well, Mandela took care of that. Once the great peace lover, the prodigal hero was released in 1990. It wasn't that many years later before I got to see plenty of his followers in action. In fact, one fine night, ten years later, I got to see them burn our farm. They had been burning out our neighbors, periodically, chasing them from their land, or worse, but as a kid—you know how kids are—it could never happen to you . . ."

Dalia stared at his face, transfixed. He was no longer with her on that bed. He was back in the hell inside his mind. "But being a kid doesn't stop awful things from happening, regardless of your happy little dreams. One night, as my father and I were returning from the fields, I thought that my mother had left on all the lights in the house and barns. *Will father be mad!* I thought. He was a frugal man, to say the least. Then my father started running. I tried to keep up but he moved faster than I'd ever seen, screaming in our language, scaring me so badly I tripped. I came up with soil in my mouth and the tears starting, not knowing why. Then my father was past the gate and three men with machetes were hacking at him as he tried to put up his arms . . . but then, his arms were gone and soon, his head . . ."

Dalia was used to brutal men. Hezbollah bred them like rabbits. But the face of this handsome, urbane individual was a mask worthy of the devil. She hardly breathed.

"I hid," Sydney continued in a voice that came from the grave. "When nothing was left but smoke clouds and the cries of burned animals, I walked through the gate. My father was in pieces. The rest of my family was strewn, like so much rubbish, over the front porch and on the smoldering earth where the house had sat.

"I wandered back to that gate. Tears in my eyes made the flickering fires magical, like a kaleidoscope." His smile was ghostlike. "Isn't that funny—at a time like that a kid sees magic and almost beauty. Near my father, a man was struggling to get up. My father was a strong man and must have hurt him, somehow. His head was off to one side and he was tottering. His eyes were very white compared to the rest of his blackness. I thought he was asking for help, but I'm not sure. His body smelled of stale perspiration and his clothes reeked of death's odors. I took a rock and knocked him on his back, jumped on his chest, and beat and pounded his head until it was jelly. There was a stench from his urine and brain, I can still remember."

Sydney lay back. Suddenly his eyes regained their focus. For a moment, he stared at Dalia in the confused fashion of someone awakened from a deep sleep. He patted her hand but his smile never reached his eyes. "I do go on, don't I? I need another cigarette—one's usually the limit."

They both lay there quietly. There were no more words.

Soon, they slept.

***

The next day they lolled around the pool, dipping frequently because the air was like a hot towel wreathing their bodies. Both were strong swimmers but the pool was small and, as the day progressed, bobbing children impeded any such activity. Tired of the mid-afternoon tumult, they retired to his room and made love with the pungent odor of chlorine strong upon their bodies. Later they returned to the same little restaurant and the same wine. Since they were the only two dining, the waitress smiled and said, "Y'all gonna eat this tahm?" Laughing, they agreed. After cappuccinos rich with towering foam, Sydney over-tipped the friendly girl and they made love again, this time in Dalia's room.

As Sydney returned from the bathroom he said, "Now let's hear your story. Only fair."

Dalia sprawled crosswise on the bed. Shadow from the subdued bathroom light rounded her buns to perfection. She wiggled, further adding to the enticement.

"Don't distract me." He sat on the edge of the bed, spread his arms back for balance, and set his mouth, waiting.

"I am from a rich family . . . " Dalia began. "Lebanon was a wondrous place for a child, before we became a political junkyard. Even after our civil war, my family and others enjoyed continued prosperity, as did our friends. Then Syria fell apart and without their economy supporting us, we lost everything. In 2005, my father hanged himself one morning, and then, our family disintegrated. I was five.

But I was lucky. A favorite uncle, who still made good after the Syrians left, sent me away to school in America." She sighed. "I think I need a cigarette, although forgive me if I cough. I haven't smoked since college."

He lit one for her and true to her word, she *coughed* with the first drag. "See?" She held the glowing end at arm's length and reached over to lay it in the ashtray. Rolling over so that her breasts lay exposed, Dalia looked up at Sydney.

Apparently, he awaited the rest of her story.

Oh well, she thought, *I tried.* "Naturally, I became radicalized. At home, my family was conservative but in America, even rich kids hated their own wealth. It was crazy . . . but I loved it. Demonstrations; threatening the college administration if they didn't do more and more stupid things; even terrorizing the Jews at the Hillel booths—God it was fun! But I think I need a water." She took a Pellegrino from the small refrigerator, handing him another. "So, although I was Christian, I fell in love with the plight of the poor Palestinians and ended up hating Israel although I knew nothing about it." She took a long pull of the water, then added, "And I hated the United States for supporting them." Dalia, dropped back on the bed and spun onto her side, bracing her head on her left arm. Batting her lashes, she leaned toward Sydney's face. And here we are," she laughed.

He touched her cheek. "You don't sound like a fanatic."

Dalia's full lips compressed as she absorbed his comment. After a moment, she said, "I'm probably not. Hezbollah and the Palestinians are Neanderthal woman haters and killers, and Israel does more good than not. I guess I'm just bored, if I really think about it."

"Bored enough to kill, obviously."

"Sure. It's exciting as long as it's no one I like . . . and maybe even then. Who knows? Sometimes I wonder about myself. Am I sick?"

His arms cradled her so hard that her breath flew from her lungs. Forcing Dalia down as he flattened his pelvis against hers, Sydney whispered softly, "Isn't this entire world?"

CHAPTER 17 NO SOCIAL DISTANCE

The two rangers were back in Arthur Krause's extravagant office. As they sat facing their slightly overweight friend, Stedmier studied the family pictures proudly arrayed before him. *Kids, much bigger than daddy, and a wife—whoo—that's somethin'.* Unkindly, he thought, *wonder if it was his money? Nah, they were married out of college and he wasn't a leading authority back then. An' this Jew-boy is a real sweetheart on top a' that so, sheet, he deserves it all an' more.* Stedmier couldn't avoid seeing all the certificates and awards framed on the wall as well. And next to the antique roll-top desk, a five-foot flowering plant in full bloom.

"...definitely focus on Pioneer and its two neighbors, Ashcroft and Carlin," Krause was saying.

Stedmier made up for his failure to hear the last part by hyper-focusing.

Flynn saved him. "Sure, Arthur, tha's the way it looks from thet circled area. So how duh we protect it?"

Stedmier leaned toward the oil expert. "An' catch those bast'uds?"

Krause concentrated, blinking his eyes rapidly. Then he nodded. "Well, if they're not using an atomic bomb—and let's suppose they're not—they're going to need a lot of explosives. You might set up roadblocks to check any trucks coming in—"

"And if they buy 'em here," broke in Stedmier, "we cover all the places that sell it in the Midland-Odessa area.

Since the slowdown, theh ain't as many dealers as before. Shouldn' be too tough."

"I'll get some men on it right away," said Flynn.

Stedmier nodded. "An' question our informers about any strangers askin' questions. An' remember them boys over at the sites. Ask 'em about poor ol' Grissom being around

recently an' who he might'a been with. With any luck, mebbe we get ourselves some descriptions."

Flynn's heavy eyebrows lowered. "Hey, Dave boy, you ain't getting' a little senile at your tenda years? You, me an' Ahtie already talked 'bout this. Got ma men on it fer 'bout a day, already."

Stedmier smiled. "Yeah, guess ah'm losin't it. Hard ta keep up all the balls we're jugglin'. They heard anything yet?"

"Hey," said Flynn, "you sounding like headquarters now. You been up theh too long, boy. Give 'em some time. Don' tell me yuh forgot that field work is slow an' steady?"

"Yup," agreed Stedmier. "Guess I'm jus' a little anxious, what with a couple a miles a the country possibly blowin' up. Ahtie, mebbe you kin figure something else they might use ta cause those wells ta explode. Like some chemical in the water or somethin'. You the expert."

"Well, sodium and potassium explode in water and wells use a lot of water." Krause wrinkled his nose. "No. It would take truckloads and there's nowhere around here that you could find that much. And, that stuff is too dangerous to transport in quantity from farther away." He pushed back his chair and stood. "Look, you guys have plenty to do. I'll talk to some of my colleagues—strictly hypothetically—and see what they come up with. No guarantees. Meantime, you both better get going."

Stedmier rose. "You ain't jus' kidding, Ahtie. Like yestaday. C'mon, Toby. We gotta git on this."

Flynn rose, grabbing for his hat. "Right with yuh, hawse. Catch ya later, Ahtie. Yuh call, yuh got anything."

"You got it." Krause was already consulting his Rolodex. "Good luck, gentlemen."

Stedmier turned at the door. "Don' know 'bout the 'gennelmen' thing, but we shore gonna need it." The rangers were out before Krause had located the first name to call.

***

Dalia's hairbrush worked through long strands of black hair, releasing them as she followed through with each stroke. She looked at Sydney through the mirror. "Are you planning to tell me what you've said you would for the past three days, or am I still not entitled?" Her voice held an edge Sydney hadn't heard during their past few days of intimacy.

"You're right." He sat on the bed behind her. His face and eyes were expressionless. "Not easy to share . . . always work alone . . . sorry."

She turned. "I understand. You work alone. But now you aren't. Unless you either want me out . . . or plan to kill me."

Sydney's chest was bare. Scars showed white against the sunburn from their day at the pool. The already substantial size of his chest increased as he drew in a deep breath. Once his mind was made up, the tall man's full lips drew back. His teeth glowed in the strong light near her mirror. "It was never about sabotage—at least not through explosives."

Her dark eyes flashed. A harsh edge infused her normally sultry voice. "I gathered that much. Here it is days from the mysterious 'weekend' and still no preparations or signs of devices, so please don't treat me like a child . . . or an imbecile."

His long finger warded off her anger. "You're right, I'm sorry."

Closing her lids slightly, Dalia's face relaxed. "All right. Accepted."

"You remember that Wuhan epidemic unleashed by the Chinese in 2020? Well, I have about six canisters of its big brother."

Although her heart throbbed in her chest, Dalia fought for impassivity. *This is what you let yourself in for when you committed,* she told herself.

"Authorities are going to assume that 'sabotage' will be a physical attack on the fracking operation, but that was never the case with this mission. Wuhan tied up the Americans for a ridiculously long time. The news here was filled with rising fatalities and everyone had a thousand medical opinions blaring at them, so they didn't know what to believe. They were paralyzed. Businesses went under; people reported each other; state leaders panicked; governors mandated the shot and politics had a field day allocating blame."

"I know," said Dalia. "I was there, at school. It was like

martial law. No classes; no socializing; no more than six in areas that could accommodate a hundred—"

"Exactly." Sydney reached for a Hetfield, ignoring the non-smoking sign near Dalia. *By the time we're through*, he thought, *smoking will be the least of my transgressions.* He drew the smoke in deep, releasing it away from her face. In a detached voice he said, "From what I understand, many will die—and not just oldsters in nursing homes." His eyes searched hers. "Can you accept that?"

Dalia wished for a cigarette, too, but rejected the idea. Instead. she looked through the gauze-like inner curtain. Beyond, the pool area and its occupants were visible in dreamlike opaqueness. The effect was to amplify their sounds of exuberance. *Mass assassination. I should be prepared—but am I? Am I really one of those maniacs who straps on a bomb and kills children in a nursery?*

Reading her thoughts, he said, "Most will survive. This country is very well prepared and the area will quickly be quarantined, *but . . .* certainly more than a few will die." He puffed calmly, following the smoke tendrils with his eyes. "Had I not developed feelings for you, this would have stayed my secret until the exact moment. Being proficient at what I do, it was prudent to keep you in the dark."

"And if I didn't remain in the dark—?" she ventured.

The freezing look in his eyes—the one that had terrified her on the occasions when Sydney threatened her and Al-Musawi—was the only answer Dalia needed. When his stormy look dissipated, like a small cloud in a large sky, he answered, "I would have asked you to leave the country. I knew you wouldn't betray me because . . . " he calmly stubbed the cigarette, "in my business that's a formula for disaster."

"Like Grissom?"

He stared into her eyes. "Yes, like Grissom. I don't *ever* leave loose ends."

The dark-haired woman reached for his neck. "Come here. I would never betray you . . . and, whatever, God help me, I'm in all the way."

***

Dalia finished her dinner and sat thinking in silence. The restaurant was nearly empty and the friendly waitress was taking a large order from a family of five across the room. "Now I know why you left those plans and the phone."

Sydney was about to sip, but held his wine glass close to his mouth as he anticipated her theory.

"Because if the authorities get wind of it, the maps will confirm that the sabotage will be at the wells."

Nodding, he sipped. "Yes, and just to help them," he winked, "I circled a location right near the biggest operation. Pioneer."

Dalia's smooth forehead furrowed. "But why the phone?"

"The middleman—and I hate every one of them in this line of work—will be discovered, you see. I neglected to use an untraceable phone. He will gladly reveal what he knows, because he has no loyalties."

"Ah," Dalia toasted, "the authorities—"

"Texas Rangers, I would think."

"So, Sydney, the Texas Rangers will confirm sabotage

and, since all the go-between knows is that poor Harv was hired as a guide to the fields, the wells must be the target." She raised her glass higher. "That is incredible," she said aloud. Aware that her voice had risen, Dalia peered around to determine if anyone had heard.

The waitress was still clarifying orders from the couple's three youngsters, her pen flying to keep up with their changing minds. Satisfied, Dalia turned back. "A question. Why did we spend hours around the water plant?"

"Have you ever heard of red herrings?"

Dalia's forehead revealed a delicate wrinkle or two. "Of course."

Her lover smiled. "Well, what will our rangers make of the fact that we also checked out the city's water supply?"

Eyes glowing with respect, Dalia exclaimed, but quietly this time, "Ha. They won't know if our target might be their city water or the wells!"

Sydney calmly sipped his remaining wine. "Did you happen to notice the markings on the base of the maps?"

"Why, no."

"They reference the U.S. Congress. Just to add to the confusion, why not bring in the anti-fossil energy forces, just to increase the possibilities as to who set this in motion. That shifts blame from our employers."

She could only stare in admiration at the perfectly calm man as he finished his wine. After a moment, her curiosity returned. "And one more."

"Anything for you."

"Why do you keep mentioning this weekend?"

The tall man straightened in his chair. "There's no

excitement in life if there is no mystery, my dear."

"Okay, but just tell me one thing and I promise . . . no more questions." Her arched toes rubbed along Sydney's shin.

With widening eyes, he said, "How can I refuse?"

"*Where* will this happen this weekend?" She rubbed harder up and down the length of his leg until her bare foot found his crotch.

Sydney bent to fondle her ankle, then moved on to her calf. "Do you like country music, my dear?" Before the frowning woman could answer, he whispered, "Let's go."

CHAPTER 18 RANGERS TO THE RESCUE

Stedmier hung up the phone.

"The brass?" asked Flynn.

"Yeah. 'How's it goin'; any leads; any witnesses?'" Stedmier's mimicking ended in a downright snort. "The usual questions with no answers. Hand me over a donut, will yuh? Yuh know as well as I do tha's the brass for yuh."

Flynn studied the donut clutched in his fingers.

"Hey, give it over. Yuh alreaduh had three."

"Yeah, yuh right," said the heavy ranger. "Here." He handed over the box. "So yuh tol' 'em we got a coupla leads?"

"The usual B.S." Stedmier took a bite. "Hey, this is good but I don' wanna look like you." He bit the frosted circle nearly in half and slid the box back. "Yeah, we got leads, but not much to go on. A foreman named Mike, at Pioneer, who knew Grissom thinks he saw a blond guy, a good-looking black-haired woman and an ugly brown guy with a beard."

"Well, we sure know who the ugly guy was," said Flynn.

"More'n likely, but the descriptions we got from that guy at the frackin' site are too vague fuh locatin' th' others, Toby."

Making a *clucking* sound, Flynn shook his heavy head. "An' aside from that, the resta my boys got little ta nothin'. No explosives sold between here an' Odessa, or fifty miles past. Be easy ta identify, cause drillin' ain't begun yet. Two other witnesses noticed a Mercedes—they don't splash aroun' those sites normally. We checked out Hertz, Sted. They th' only ones have luxury cars for rent."

"Yeah?"

"The license was a phony, natchally, an' nobody remembers much. Tough when we ain't got no pitures fa them tuh I.D. Nobody notices nobody, now'days , unless yuh got two heads . . . or yuh tits is showin'.'"

"Yuh got Hertz goin' through their records, Toby? Those suspects shore needed some otha' wheels."

Flynn cracked his knuckles. The *pop* filled his office. "Jeez, why do I do thet? It hurts! Ana'way, they musta showed fake licenses . . ."

Stedmier shrugged. "Yeah, I know. No way tuh tell 'less every legit car is turned in. As busy as we' gettin' here in town, some cahs may be out for weeks. Hertz will try callin' an' verafyin' all customuhs, but they don' wan' everyone pissed off. Same with the otha' rental places."

"Not when we cain't tell 'em why. I cain't blame 'em," Flynn said, shaking his head. "But we sure cain't be mentionin' po-tential terrerists. Start a fuckin' panic, Sted. Cain't do that."

.

Stedmier rose, gazing at the parking lot. He smacked the blind. It *crackled.* "So, where the fuck ah we?"

Flynn looked up. "Hey, tha's a ol' joke, Sted. 'Long lost tribe . . .'"

Stedmier's thin lips registered no humor. "Yeah. On us. An' lots' a innocent citizens if'n we don' catch a break."

***

A half hour later there was a call from Krause. "What yuh got, Ahtie?" said Flynn. "Nothing much, Toby. Ask twenty eggheads, you get twenty-two answers. Long and the short, outside of flooding the water supply with oil so the surface burns, or volatile metals—which it would take a railroad car's worth—and aside from a couple of other ideas that would be appropriate for Flash Gordon or Buck Rogers, no one came up with anything."

Flynn shook his head toward an expectant Stedmier. "Well, yuh could onla' try," Flynn said into the phone.

Toby," said Krause, "are you sure there's nothing else? Something's still bothering me. Did they go anywhere else? With no supplies, I don't see how they can take out those wells. Is it possible there's dynamite or some other explosives already at the site?"

Flynn stared at the phone as if it was a live grenade. "Jeez, we nevuh thought sumthin' could be hidden in all thet huge equipment thet ain't been used yet. Mebbe months ago someone brought the stuff in when th' sites was practically deserted. Lot'ta thet heavy stuff jus' sat there. Thanks, Ahtie. No wonda ya make the big bucks! We'll check an' git back t'yuh."

As Flynn slammed the phone, Stemier said, "What? What, for god sakes, Toby?"

Flynn was already yelling into the other phone. "Stevens, git the boys in here. We got a shitload of searchin' tuh do, an' I don' know hah much time we have. So don' nobody plan on goin' home till it's as dahk at night as a penguin's asshole."

***

Word spread quickly in a small city like Midland. Before long, talk over the fences and even in the barbershops was that the rangers were swarming around all the heavy equipment at the prospective fracking sites. Operators were called back to manage monster blenders, gigantic frac pumps and colossal mobile storage units. The *hum* of machinery saturated the air for two days well into the nights. That is when Stedmier, standing near a water truck whose wheels reached higher than his six-foot-two frame, called it off. Then he treated those involved to beers at a local watering hole. The bar was a favorite ranger hangout. Pictures of heroes, alive and deceased, lined the corridor to the men's room.

Walking back to the high-top, Flynn said, "Don't know we'll evuh see our own selves up there on the crapper hall a' fame, Sted, 'specially if'n we fuck this up."

Too depressed to say much, the two rangers hoisted their Ziegenbock Amber lagers and munched peanuts.

A voice rose from behind them. "Hey, Rangers, how y'all doin'?" The young man was about nineteen, with permanent acne and hair plastered along his forehead. He peeked from under a ten-gallon.

Oh shit, thought Stedmier, *jus' wha' I need. A fuckin' fan.* "Doin' fahn, son," he managed a sleepy-eyed smile. "An' you?"

"Fair to middlin', Ranger." The youth scratched under his hat, nearly toppling it off. "I hear you fellahs been doing a lot of checking on equipment ovah them sites— don' know why, an' it's none a mah business, but ma uncle Sandy works over at Pioneer. Said rangers was askin' 'bout a Mercedes a few days ago."

Despite his discouragement and one-too-many brews, Stedmier's radar honed in. "Yup," he said, "what yuh got, son?"

"Well, I work ovuh at City Water Treatment, an' a few days ago I see this big Mercedes jus' windin' in an' out, takin' it all in. Not that it's so damn much to take in but they're goin' slow as yuh please. Me an' the boys was laugin' that when yuh got a car like that there's lot bettuh shit to do than watchin' aerator fountains an' snappin' turtles. Damned if they didn' do that for near an hour."

Flynn, too, was suddenly alert. "Did yuh see ana'one in it?"

"Nah, too far."

Just then, a good-looking girl with a red bandana came over. "Yuh gonna introduce me to the rangers, Randy?" She was all of seventeen and stared directly at Stedmier.

Embarrassed, Stedmier introduced himself and Flynn, both trying hard to ignore her spectacular cleavage. As the girl's gaze intensified, Stedmier said, "We bettuh git goin', Flynn."

Her boyfriend was in full agreement and grabbed her by the elbow. "See yuh, Rangers," he said, turning angrily toward the protesting girl.

Flynn tipped his beer bottle till there was none left. His round cheeks reared under his eyes. "Yuh still got it, Sted," he laughed.

"Yeah, great. Tha's jus' what ah need. But how 'bout thet treatment plant tour? Why fool aroun' with drink'n water? Huh, Toby?"

Flynn dug for his car keys. They gleamed in the light from a Budweiser sign. "Don' know, Sted. Bettuh git back an' see Ahtie fust thing."

Stedmier pushed open the very new, old-fashioned saloon swinging doors. "You are sure right. Fus' thing."

***

"See, that's what was bothering me," said Krause. He was diminutive by comparison to his oversized desk. He shook his head. "Yeah, that was what I was afraid of." The petroleum expert had been nodding at the puzzle pieces floating around inside his head, without saying a perceptible word to the two others in his office. Sometimes he leaned back and stared up at the ceiling like he was meditating. Every time his eyes sparkled, the rangers got ready for him to break out of his contemplation, only to see him settle back into the mold of his own thoughts.

Staring at the man, Stedmier said, "*Ahtie,* what the hell ah you afraid of? Mind sharing? It sure would be he'pful."

Flynn just shook his head. "Mebbe by lunch he'll get tuh it."

Like an awakened sleepwalker, Krause blinked. "Oh yes. Sorry, it's just so—"

"What?" growled Stedmeir. "I'm gonna—"

"What if it's chemical . . . or biological?"

Flynn's eyes widened. "Jeez."

No need fer tons of explosives," breathed out Stedmier. "Just a coupl'a test tubes in yuh pocket."

"Carry 'em ana'where," added Flynn.

Stedmier ran long fingers across his broad forehead. "Use 'em ana'where . . . like the water supply,"

Arthur Krause closed his eyes. "Like the water supply," he echoed. "I'd better start asking about water transmitted bacteria, hadn't I?"

"Yeah," both rangers repeated simultaneously. "Guess, yuh bettuh."

***

Sandy Hill in Ottawa is a trendy area of brew pubs, bookstores and coffee houses, suitable for a college town. Fashi made his way through a crowd of students belonging to the University of Ottawa. They ranged from pristine youths dressed in summer casual high fashion to Africans sporting the flamboyant colors of their lands. Like students everywhere, their aura of ebullience was born of the certitude that opportunities ahead were unlimited.

To Fashi, their carefree naiveté was an irritant as he moved along Henderson Avenue toward the modest homes subdivided for student housing. Here, the demeanor was less boisterous; the apparel more utilitarian.

He knocked at the back door of an especially chopped up house with foreign flags decorating its windows. A dark youth of twenty bowed him in. "Welcome, we have been expecting you. My name is Hassan."

Sprawled underwear, t-shirts and sweaters littered the floor around the sparse furniture. Shoes peeped out from beneath a half-opened convertible sofa. White stuffing erupted from the cushion of an armchair, while a tower of books balanced precariously upon a small table. Beneath it sat the residue of French fries and an empty bun on a paper plate. The sink, filled with dishes, was crowned by a crusty pan whose handle thrust straight up. A nearby electric burner peeked from behind a barricade of milk cartons and soup cans.

"Sorry," said Hassan, "but with classes and everything—"

"That's all right," said Fashi. "Sudden notice and all that." Hassan had a long face and wide ears. His smile unified all areas with pleasant charm. "Yes . . . sudden notice." He yanked open the sofa bed. It relented with a tortured *creak.* "You will sleep here. I'll be upstairs with a friend." The same smile made the nature of his 'friendship' apparent to Fashi.

Hassan said, "We will travel to the border tomorrow morning. It is not far and security around New York is a joke."

"I have a student visa," ventured Fashi.

"Oh, that is easy. We go back and forth all the time. Then we will use a border crossing. They know us all and one more along with us won't make a difference." He shrugged. "They won't care ."

Fashi pulled off his pack.

"Just throw it on the bed. Got a clean towel in the bathroom—it's tiny so watch your head—and use any of my things you need. There's a key under the flower pot and plenty of good places to eat if you go back up Henderson a few blocks. Gotta go. See you about 7:30 tomorrow."

Hassan was gone before Fashi could thank him.

CHAPTER 19 ENTER THE F.B.I.

The J. Edgar Hoover building sprawls along Pennsylvania Avenue for a full block. On its upper levels, policy is made and coordination with the Attorney General's office is accomplished in a conference room adjacent to the office of the Director of the Federal Bureau of Investigation. This morning, the assistant heads of both agencies were poring over a file initiated by the F.B.I. Director. Its urgency curtailed their normal leisurely breakfast planning session.

"Texas Rangers came up with a good one here," said the Deputy Assistant Attorney General. He was a small man whose narrow shoulders compressed when he talked. "Possible sabotage of oil facilities in Texas. Fracking as a matter of fact."

"I thought that was over and done after Trump," said his far larger F.B.I. counterpart, whose robust chest seemed to swell out his conventional gray jacket.

"No, Jim. Not with the new president. He's hot for it. Turned out he likes a lot of Trump's ideas—just never mentioned them before."

"Well, Marshall, that sure must have pissed off the party royally. Hah, hah, what a hoot."

The AG second in command's blond eyebrows curled toward his nose. He furtively peered around. "Not so loud. The walls have ears around here."

His companion's narrow shoulders hunched and his eyes roved the large room, but its occupants were all involved in their own conversations. "Sorry. We getting this out to the Special Agent-in-Charge over in El Paso?"

"Yeah. ASAP. Could be local or foreign, or both. Let them sort it out, but I'll let my boss know we're on it. Make sure we get twice-a-day updates."

The smaller man rose, clutching the file to his chest as if it was a treasure map. "You got it, Marshall. See you later."

***

On the third floor of the Midland F.B.I. office on Spring Street, Special Agent-in-Charge, Luis Guerrera, pored over the information from headquarters. A huge smile painted his wide face. "Harry, this is like Christmas in summer: a chance to fuck around with the rangers."

His second in command, Harry Stone, was six-six of solid muscle. His jacket bulged over his chest and arms. "Well, that sounds good to me, Luis. Maybe it's a chance to take those cowboys down a peg. 'Oldest law enforcement agency in the country.' Big, fucking deal. Who cares about cattle rustlers anymore?"

Guerrero slapped down the file. "'Domestic or foreign terrorism'—that's our turf. And this sure looks like it, what with explosives and sabotage."

Stone nodded. "Right in our wheelhouse. The cowboys can't argue about that."

Guerrero, a medium sized man, moved catlike to the door. "Let's just go unannounced. That'll burn fat Flynn's ass."

Stone unwound his long frame from the chair. "Right with you, boss man."

***

"Ah knew there was a smell in the office," said Flynn, as soon as the young ranger who showed Guerrero and Stone in was out of earshot. "Thought somethin' had died in the air conditionin' vents. Hey, Guerro, see you are with thet monster a yours, Lurch."

"Fuck you, Hopalong Cassidy," said the red-faced Stone.

"We love you too," grinned Guerrero, "but this isn't a social visit."

Flynn sighed. "Yeah, ah know. Stedmier's in the john."

"Oh, the famous headquarters captain and *your* superior." Guerrero's dark eyes crinkled. "How old are you, Flynn? About fifty something? And how old is he? About thirty something? Gee, what happened?"

Stedmier entered, interrupting Flynn's reply. "Ah you babies gon'na be at it th' whole fuckin' time? It's enough we gotta work with yuh without the BS. This is serious, unless yuh don't much care 'bout th' city blowin' up. So have a coffee an' le's git tuh business."

Flynn pointed. "S'ovah there in the corner. Help yusself."

The agents obliged. "Thanks." Guerrero seated himself and waited for Stone. His eyes were serious now. "We read the file but it doesn't say much: terrorists; unknown origin; Permian Basin suspected target, blah, blah, blah. Any more to the story? C'mon now, Toby. You know we don't get all jurisdictional down here no matter what the assholes in D.C. think."

Flynn lifted his coffee, winking at Stedmier. "Yeah, Sted, fuh F.B.I., they pretty good ol' boys."

Stedmier winked back. "I'll take yuh word fuh it, Toby, though it's against muh better judgement. Seriously, this has got us a bit confused." He outlined the salient points of their investigation for the next ten minutes, Flynn interjecting when appropriate. The young ranger captain concluded with, "Our frien', Arthur Krause—"

"I know Krause," Guererro blurted. "A good man. Helped us more than once."

Stedmier nodded. "Ana'way, Ahtie thinks it could be somethin' otha than explosives, 'cause thehs no sign a' them, neither at the sights or shipped in from outside—"

"An' we think the time is close fuh wahtevuh," said Flynn. "More coffee?"

Both agents waved the suggestion off. Stone stretched his long legs nearly under Flynn's desk. "So what does your friend think?" His voice was surprisingly soft for such a large man.

"Something easy to carry . . . like biological."

"Shit," said Gurerrero.

"Or a suitcase nuke," said Stone. "Easy to smuggle in

and detonate. I don't know much about oil shale but I have to believe there's plenty of gas down there to set off a chain reaction. Anyone know?"

Flynn reached for the phone. "Don' sound too farfetched tuh me," he said. "But, what say? Let's get Ahtie in on it?" He waited a moment, then said, "Hey, Ahtie, Flynn here. Jus' hypo-thetically speakin', could somethin' nucleah set off the shale?"

They watched Flynn's face darken steadily as he listened. "Thanks. Now, we don' know nothin' fa sure. Just speculatin'. Talk ta yuh later." The ranger pressed his full lips together, rubbing his chin before speaking. "Unduh the right conditions, says Ahtie, the shale shelf could undergo spontaneous ex-othe'mic reactions."

Stedmier grimaced. "Talk English, Toby."

Flynn sighed. "Means given the right heat level—say nuclear and ox-yen--this shale could blow higher than a hawk with a hot foot."

***

Kelly Frank had flaming red hair and an insatiable thirst for fresh news. Although just out of grad school, she had landed a job with the Capital Chronicle, and was already known as an up-and-comer after only six months. As she sat with her legs crossed—a ploy that frequently got her a little extra information during interviews—Kelly noticed her editor's eyes surveying her exposed thigh. "I tell you, Fred, there is something wrong about Grossman's suicide."

Fred Goldfarb knew that a man of sixty-three, with four grandkids, shouldn't be sneaking peeks under young girls' skirts, but what could he do? Refocusing with effort, he stared into her powder blue eyes. "Kelly, the fuc—sorry, damn coroner confirmed powder burns on Grossman's fingers and the entry trajectory was consistent for his right hand—for which the fingerprints on the gun, by the way, were a perfect match. So why are you beating a dead horse?"

"Everyone said he was a rising party star. Very ambitious and fanatically dedicated to causes like global warming and green energy. Gee, Fred, he was scheduled to speak at a huge rally at the University of Texas next week . . . and he and his wife had a luxury cruise scheduled for the Fall." Kelly swept a hand through some errant strands of her hair. Multi-colored nail polish glistened in the light from the window. "Does that really sound like a man about to kill himself?"

Rolling his eyes, the editor's voice weakened. "I can't spare you. We're a small paper—"

She tilted her head. "*Please*, Fred. Just a few days to interview the wife and friends. *Please*?"

Fighting to restore his flagging manhood, Fred Goldfarb sucked up his substantial gut and growled, "One week. One week and *that's it!* Now get outta here!"

Kelly gaily chirped, "Thanks, Fred. You're a doll," and ran out.

Goldfarb's bald head approximated the shade of the Santa Suit he always wore at the paper's charity Christmas party. "I'll get even. I'm making you an *elf* this year," he barked at the empty doorway.

***

Sydney sat in the motel room's undersized armchair,

scanning Thursday's local paper.

Dalia stopped brushing her hair, glancing at him through the mirror next to the TV. "You've been reading this hick paper all week," she said. "Why?"

"Just making sure a particular event I'm interested in is running this weekend."

The dark-haired beauty rose. "Is it that?" She pointed to a full-page advertisement bordered by guitars and balloons. Pictures of mostly Latin entertainers covered the interior, superimposed upon a large band shell and sprawling audience. Ten-Gallons and sombreros abounded among the wildly enthusiastic crowd. Some hats were frozen sailing into the air.

Above it all, huge letters blasted: *"See y'all at the Annual West Texas Blowout. This Friday through Sunday."* Below, in slightly smaller print, was: *Cimarex Energy Pavilion* and smaller yet, *5514 Champions Drive, Midland, Texas.*

Sydney looked up. "Yes. That's it. They usually get a few hundred thousand. And Sunday is the big finale—biggest stars, biggest crowds."

"That's when *we'll* be there?"

Sydney closed the paper, reaching his arms out for her. "That's when we'll be there."

CHAPTER 20 150 NANOMETERS

Stedmier sat at the conference table at local Ranger headquarters. By mutual agreement, Guerrero and the F.B.I. would cooperate jointly, without jurisdictional squabbling—a situation unique to Texas as well as to the mutual respect the two agencies had for one another. It was also why Texans were able to solve crimes more efficiently and rapidly than other jurisdictions. Maps of Midland and vicinity hung along one full wall. Prominent were locations of all local fracking operations, although many were still not operational.

"S'long as there's equipment an' intact wells," explained Stedmier, "we gotta keep it *all* under surveillance, 'cause underneath, they *all* connect to the shale bed."

"Agreed," said Guerrero as he studied a map which gently flapped in the air conditioning currents. "One blast anywhere and there's a chain reaction."

Flynn leaned back in his chair and yelled out the door, "Would one a you guys brang us more tape. We kin goddamn afford it." A nervous rookie hurried in, taping the bottoms of the maps and ducking back out.

"Hell of a lot of territory," commented Stone.

Flynn shook his head. "And the fuckin' water plant, too. Where we gonna git the manpower?"

Stedmier set his jaw. "We gonna git everyone we kin from the whole damn state. Forget speed traps an' bullshit an' git the hell down here, pronto—that's what I'm gonna tell 'em. An' you kin bet your ass they will."

Guerrero nodded to Stone. "This is one *big fucking deal!* Get on that phone, man. We need to get everyone they can spare here. I'll call our guys in Oklahoma and Arizona and see what they can send. If that's not enough, I'll go all the way up to the Deputy Assistant Director." He thrust out of his chair like his pants were on fire.

Already digging for his phone, Stone followed. Both left without a word.

***

Four hours later, they were all back. Stedmier stood before the largest map. Most of the others had been taken down. "We need parameters 'roun all the areas marked in yellow. In red are th' vantage points where our people should be stationed to git a clear view of the subject areas. Blue are the routes of rovin' cahs, coordinating information an' visually covering peripheral areas borderin' the primary sites. We have forty or more men committed, startin' late tonight—"

"We've got thirty-two, so far," said Stone. "Probably at least ten more."

Stedmier nodded. "Tha's great, Stone. 'Course if yuh could rustle up a few more, wouldn't hurt. Damn big amount tuh cover."

"I'm working on it," said Guerrero, "but manpower is stretched as it is, so we're lucky to get that many."

Flynn raised his hands. "Hey, we' damn grateful yuh could come up with this many, so fast."

"Sure," said Stedmier, "don' git me wrong. Ahm jus' edgy. What yuh think a the plan?"

Guerrero squinted up at the map again. "Should do the job. What about barricades?"

"Mebbe at key points," said Flynn, "but it'd take fo-evah tuh round up enough for all that acreage."

"Yeah, you're right," agreed Guerrero. "But maybe for about two hundred feet each side of the red areas."

Stedmier rose. "Good idea. An' dogs. Won't be any good at sniffin' out nukes, but kin sure help in chasin' down perps. An' we got a couple a state helicoptuhs, too." He glanced at his watch. "The guys'll be arrivin' anytime now. Gotta git down an' start coordinatin'. Toby?"

"Right with yuh," said Flynn.

Guerrero said, "Us, too. Our guys have been told to follow your suggestions—can't call them 'orders.' Our agents from outside the area wouldn't go for that."

"'Corse not," said Stedmier. "Thanks fer the help. Ain't no egos at a time like this."

Stone snapped his fingers. "Hey, what about that water plant?"

Flynn moved toward the coffee. "It's a city issue. They gonna use their cops tuh patrol. Any trouble, we all gonna be in radio contact."

Guerrero fished his car keys from a pocket. "Sounds good. Stay in touch, and good luck." With a brief wave, the F.B.I. agents left.

***

The trip across the United States border was a piece of cake, just as Hassan had promised. The pleasant youth who provided him with housing had three friends to take Fashi on the one-hour drive. Fashi's casual clothes, purchased the afternoon before at a highly popular student store, blended perfectly with those of his companions.

Just another group of kids shopping in the U.S., assumed the guard as he perfunctorily scanned their visas at the Ogdensburg, New York crossing. Once over, the jovial group dropped the Iranian at the Greyhound pick up point. None had the slightest idea that he wasn't visiting relatives in Albany.

***

It was early Friday when Fashi caught the bus into Manhattan. From there he'd determine the fastest way south. *I am on my own now,* he thought, as the upstate New York countryside flew by. He found New York to be surprisingly pretty. Beautiful country with hills and lakes. Not at all what he had imagined. It wasn't until Westchester that traffic began to increase. By the time he got to Bronx, he realized that the city wasn't anything like upstate. Or, like anywhere else he had ever been before.

Once the ordeal of catching a plane to Dallas was overcome, Fashi's brain immediately occupied itself with his next problem: who to contact? Neither officials in Iran nor Canada had been extremely helpful. All seemed to be guessing. Some thought the F.B.I.; others the Texas Rangers; others the military or National Guard. It was apparent to the bright young lieutenant that no one really had the vaguest idea.

What constantly haunted Fashi was that the killers had had days already. *How much time do I have? Maybe it's happening right now. Maybe in an hour.* He knew the

Council was depending on him. Despite the cool air blowing down, Fashi felt flushed. *If I let this happen, America will demolish my country . . . my family . . . my friends.* He had no concerns for the Supreme Leader or his Guardian Council because, as Fashi had confided to his friends in private, "They are just a bunch of geriatric cases keeping our country in the Middle Ages."

The young lieutenant reviewed his options as the seatbelt sign flashed. *First I get to Midland; next I contact whoever is the most important law enforcement. When I get there, I can always ask who people respect the most—that's a good start.* Fashi settled back as the wheels of the plane hit the ground. The engines let out a deafening *growl* as the pilot reversed momentum.

***

Late Friday, Flynn's car radio blasted as he rode home for a break. "Two unauthorized persons climbing the fence at the north end of the water plant." A moment later the voice *crackled* back on. "Now approaching northernmost water purification tanks. Preparing to intercept."

The heavy ranger wheeled his vehicle around and was halfway toward Midland Drive when the same voice said: "Abort. Just some kids sneaking in to watch the aerators. Repeat, abort. Just a couple of now very scared kids." The voice chuckled. "You should'a seen their faces when four cars came screaming up. They were springing their own water faster than the fountains."

Red faced, Flynn yanked up his mike. "If you're the local cops, this ain't a funny situ-ation. Do you read me?

You're under us for the time being, so cut the friggin' humor an' *git back tuh your posts—all a' you!"*

Flynn's chubby face creased in a grin as the radio went immediately dead. He just couldn't help himself. "Spurting more than the aerators. Tha's good."

***

Quite early on Saturday, Stedmier's phone rang as he was shaving. He grabbed a towel and then picked up the receiver. "Stedmier."

"Our team over at Pioneer spotted a vehicle cruising around the heavy fracking equipment. Right now they're at the Frac Pumps. We're moving in."

"Y'all go. Be careful. I'll be there in twen'y." The tall ranger stopped shaving, wiped the foam off and grabbed his jacket as he yanked open the door to his motel room. He, too, was stopped a few minutes later as he cleared the motel parking lot.

"Everyone stand down," said the radio. "Just a family from Ohio takin' an early tour. We should'a run those barricades clear across the damn sites—sorry, Captain."

"S'all right," responded Stedmier. "We should'a run the fuckin' barricades all the way 'round."

"Thanks, Captain," laughed the voice. "Bettuh luck next time."

"Here's hopin'." Stedmier broke the connection.

***

At 10:00 they still had nothing.

Flynn's usual good humor had evaporated with a sleepless night and multiple false alarms. "I'm more jittery than a spaniel waitin' on a duck. I don' even want a donut."

Stedmier toyed with his coffee, then rubbed his red eyes. "Yeah. Know what yuh mean . . . this damn waitin' . . . not bein' able tuh do a damn thing. Hear ana'thing from Guerrero?"

"Nothin,'" Flynn answered. "Same as us. He did round up a few more guys tuh help."

Stedmier looked at the digital clock on Flynn's desk. It had barely moved since the last time he checked it. Under its face, a small plaque on the wooden base read: *To the best Captain in the Rangers.* "Guess all we kin do is wait," he said.

***

On the American flight from Dallas to Midland, a big man with a drawl assured Fashi that, "Our Rangers are the best damn law enforcement group anywhere in the U S of A, bar none."

The sentiment was seconded by other passengers, although in less colorful terms. By the time he'd rented a car at 2:13 p.m., Fashi was perfectly clear on whom to contact. His only problem was how, without involving his country.

***

Using the TracFone he'd acquired at the airport, Fashi easily located ranger headquarters. Captain Tobias Flynn was listed at the top. The time was 2:51.

"Flynn, here," said a particularly impatient voice, when the chain of command finally determined that the caller would talk to Flynn and none other. "Not meanin' tuh be rude but I'm real busy so this better be damn impo'tant."

"Are you so busy with a possible attempt on your oil fields?"

The impatience in Flynn's voice changed to caution. "Could be. Where'd yuh hear thet?"

"Not over the phone. We must meet. I assure you my information is, as you Americans say, a game changer."

Flynn's right hand fluttered toward the young ranger near his desk. "Git a trace on this," he whispered. *This jokuh knows his stuff.* "Okay, so where we gon'na meet an' when? Ahm at-yuh service."

"I want you to know I do not plan to be interrogated. I have no other information except what I tell you and two very important pictures. Aside from that, I have nothing of use to you and I assure, I am not part of whatever is going to happen . . . if anything even does. It is important that my sources are strictly kept out of this for serious diplomatic reasons. If I do not have your assurances, this call and my assistance are over, *now*."

I believe the son-of-a bitch, thought Flynn. *Sounds like a pro. Ah'll discuss it with Sted, but this is on me.* The bulky ranger took a breath. "Aw right. A'hm takin' yuh at yuh word, friend. Don' know why, but I am. Kin ah bring in m'ah partner. He's a good man, an' my superior?"

"I prefer not. What I give you, you are welcome to share, but I want to keep this meeting to one. Unless you prefer him—"

"In this jurisdiction, a'hm the guy."

Fashi had to smile. *Everyone is jealous of their territory. No different here than at home.* He also hoped he'd correctly understand the drawl in every word these Texan officers spoke. "Then I will call in an hour. I am disposing of my phone immediately," he reported.

"Save yusself the money. You got m'ah word."

As he left, Fashi dropped the phone in a nearby trash container.

***

It was a strange night in Midland. Seldom seen rain turned the pavements into mirrors reflecting the gaudy lights of liquor stores and all-night eateries. Flynn recognized at least three hookers that he had run in during his long career—or, maybe, their daughters. Shadowy figures slithered in and out of doorways peddling their products, making book, or collecting money from their girls.

Although hardened to life on the streets, the ranger felt tingles of apprehension. *Sheet, why'd he pick here? A'hm too young ta quit but I shore as hell wanna' collect a pension someday. How'd he even know 'bout this shithole?*

The address he'd been given was an alley in between two shops boarded by corrugated covers. The thin passage looked hazy in the sparse light, with skeletal fire escapes dangling along its length. Twisted plastic bags flopped like translucent corpses out of garbage cans. Rain rivulets crept randomly along the alley's gouged surface like tentacles of an underground beast.

As he left his car, Flynn's hand crawled toward his holster. *What have I gottin' myself inta? I didn't even tell Sted. Damn m'ah stupid code a honor.*

Farther down, he made his way to a flashlight beam

illuminating the murky air. A shadow separated from the gritty buildings. "Captain?"

"Yeah." Flynn's hand caressed the leather of his holster.

"No worries," said the soft voice. "I mean no harm."

Last time I heard that," thought Flynn, *I got two bullets fer m'ah trouble.*

The man was taller than Flynn and ramrod straight. "Call me Joe," said Fashi. "I chose this area because I could see anyone approaching and a large group of law enforcement would send the neighborhood scattering, giving me an easy escape."

"Good thinkin', 'Joe'. Yuh sure don't sound like a 'Joe,' but who'm I tuh say?" Flynn relaxed. *This doesn't feel like an assassination, or ah'd be dead already.*

"I've been told that you rangers are honorable men. You kept your word about being alone, so I determine you are both honorable and brave and I am glad of that. I didn't come here to hurt anyone."

"Glad ta hear it, Joe. Me neither." Flynn's large stomach rose and fell with a huge breath. "What'cha got fer me?"

From beneath his shirt, Fashi removed the envelope that he had guarded so carefully. "I am afraid there may not be much time. It was difficult getting across this large country. I hadn't anticipated—"

"Okay, Joe, yuh here now an' if'n there ain't much time," Flynn gave his patented grin, "we bettuh git at it."

Fashi approached, palms open toward Flynn. "Yes. I believe that the people you are after have some or all biological weapons."

"What the—you ain't shittin' me?" Flynn's already prominent eyes protruded further. "M'ah, God. Thet's worse than we figured. What is it?"

"A more advanced strain of what we called 'Covid' in twenty-twenty."

"Advanced?"

"It spreads faster and is significantly more deadly."

"Fuckin' great. *My achin' Uncle Humphrey!*"

Fashi shook his head. "What?"

"Neva' mind. Joe. Jus' a dumb expression when I cain't wrap my head 'roun' somethun'."

Fashi produced a paper from his envelope. "I have here what I believe will explain it. The primary thing to absorb is that this strain is one-hundred-fifty nanometers in diameter. The 2020 version was only one-hundred-twenty-five, which made it the largest of its time for viruses that use RNA to replicate—"

Flynn waved pudgy hands. "Whoa, sonny. You are losing this poor ol' boy. I flunked cuttin' up a frog."

"It is all on the paper. The point is that it contains even more genomes than its predecessor. That offers them even more options to replicate and their genomic proofreading system prevents mutations which could weaken it."

Flynn shook his head. " Ah kin see yuh have a real background in this, an' that makes me be'leve yuh. But if yuh don' mind," he waved the paper, "ah'll jus' give this tuh people who unnerstand it."

"As you wish, but please make haste to show it to those people you talk about. It can save many lives."

"Ah will, soon as I git back.

"Before you go," Fashi produced two photographs: One of a swarthy man, the other an attractive woman. "These are the ones we believe will carry this out. There is a third. A non-muslim, but we have no name or picture. The names of these two, if they haven't changed them, are Dalia Lavawi and Hashim-al-Musawi. Their backgrounds are inscribed on the back."

Flynn recognized the dead al-Musawi immediately from the crime scene at the airport parking lot, but saw no reason to mention it. "Yu'all pretty sure a this?"

Fashi's voice was sharp "I would not have travelled this far if I were not. But if you don't believe me, I have done the best I can."

Flynn waved his hands. "Hol' on, Joe. I 'preciate what yuh done." His heavy cheeks rode up toward his eyes. "An' who yuh with, agin?"

Fahshi's eyes were dark daggers. "Do not insult me, please. I have done what I can. I will leave you now. I cannot be involved. The implications for my country would be disastrous. If you try to detain me, I will have no choice but to kill you—I can with my hands alone, believe me, old man."

"I guess tha's why yuh chose this here spot," Flynn began, feeling for his holster, "sorry, but I really need yuh tuh come with—"

The agile young man disappeared down a side ally that Flynn hadn't noticed in the darkening haze. As the stunned ranger scrambled toward the opening, the echo of running footsteps reverberated from its gloom.

"Well, fuck me an' th' mule I came in on," he muttered. Flynn double-timed back to his car and its radio.

CHAPTER 21 SUPER SPREADER

As Flynn's vehicle sped along shining streets, the tires of his car skidded more than once. His hand was on the radio for the first ten minutes, upsetting his vehicle's stability on the slippery surface.

His first call was to Stedmier, outlining the results of his meeting with Joe. "This guy was some kinda Arab, Sted. Not surprisin' considerin' the dead one at the airport."

"An' there is a second picture, too?"

"Yeah, good lookin' hottie—*sheet, this asshole in front'a me nevuh heard muh siren!*—anaway, she's our only lead, considerin'. An' the worst, it ain't no bombs . . . it's the fucking Wuhan! Think a' it as 'Wuhan' on steroids, 'cording to our boy. Got the chemistry of it right here on the seat next'a me. He shore sounded like he knew what he was talkin' 'bout. We'll get it ta the labs, soon as ah git there in 'bout ten."

Stedmier frowned. "How's that fit with th' water plant? It ain't Ahtie's expa'tise, but he was bothered 'bout the explosives theory. Remember? An' sure seems like he was right about it being somethin' small but not explosives. This is worse cause it's even smaller an' could be used anywhere. Mebbe he kin help agin."

Flynn's eyes flashed on a slow-moving VW bug that wasn't responding. He swung wide, doubling-back fast as an oncoming RV frantically flashed its lights. "Good idea. Sheet. Ah bettuh keep tuh my drivin', or I ain't gonna be here fo' the finale."

"Be careful, Toby. I'll get the meetin' set up, pronto. Bringin' in the F.B.I. boys, too. See yuh when yuh get here."

**

The lights insidethe ranger office blazed, although the other windows in the building had been dark for hours. All the chairs of the main meeting room had been brought in, while others lined the walls, but some attendees still had to stand. While most were in uniform, some had forsaken their strictly proscribed outfits due to the hasty nature of the meeting.

F.B.I. and rangers sat side-by-side, without regard to rank or experience. A few gripped the customary coffee or soft drinks for energy. This was crash time. Rumors were at large and everyone expected the worst.

Flynn stood before them. The nighttime stubble along his chin and cheeks was something for which he ordinarily would have chewed anyone else out. The race back to the office and making rushed calls on the way had left him drained, but he fought not to let it show. "Gentlemen, we ah passin' out pictures a suspects in an' espionage plot tuh infect the whole Midland region with some kinda plague like Covid."

There was a mixture of comments and epithets even from a group as disciplined as this. A hand shot up from an F.B.I. suit. "Got any idea when?"

The heavy captain shook his head. "Not a one. We figguh soon, but that ain't much help. Sorry."

A tall ranger from the Dallas office said, "I've been assigned to the water treatment plant. Is that where this

Covid thing could be spread? In the drinking water?"

Stedmier scratched his chin. "We had a friend of ours talk to his scientific associates. Seems Covid, for you scientific sorts, doesn't pa'ticua'ly care fer filtration or disinfection thet they use there, so I'm not so sure thet's the target . . . course we cain't rule it out."

The tall Ranger from Dallas said, "Sounds like they're throwing us a lot of red herrings."

Flynn nodded, before shaking his head multiple times. "You got *that*, Freemont. We dealin' with some crafty charactuhs, much tuh mah regret."

Freemont's broad shoulders dropped. "Hate to say it, Captain, but it doesn't sound like we know where this could be, let alone when."

Stedmier stood up. His suntanned face contrasted with fierce blue eyes. "That's 'zactly right. Now thet we know th' problem, le's git working on the solution, hear me? Ain't nobody goin' home."

He looked at Guerrero, who gave him a thumbs-up. Stedmier continued to say, "Not 'til we figure out where these assholes gonna to hit us. At least we know what one a them looks like. That's half the battle." He pushed back his chair. "All you git yuh thoughts together. Ah'll git the pizzas. Le's jump on it, huh?"

***

All that was left of the pizzas was strewn boxes when young Lawson Rogers approached Flynn's desk. "Cap'n, of all the cars rented that night you asked about—"

"Huh," Flynn said, "what cahs you talkin' 'bout, Rogers?"

"At the airport—"

"Oh, yeah. Ah got it now. Mah bad."

"You have a lot on your plate, Cap'n. Anyway, sorry it took a while, but only one name and address were funny. And no such phone number."

"Great. We got the make an' license?"

"Sure do, sir. Here they are."

Flynn grabbed the paper. "This sure helps. Git ever'one rounded up an' we'll git this out. Mebbe we got somethin'. Ah'll call Commissioner Brunson tuh git the local cops on the lookout. More eyes, better chances."

***

It was past twelve when Stedmier called the group together again. Red eyes abounded and postures slouched. "Ah know its late, but we runnin' outta time. What'd you geniuses come up with? Don' wait on cer'mony, but let yuh spokesmen summarize, if yuh don' mind."

They had broken up into teams. The participants of the past hour's brainstorming had decided on groups primarily by their respective branches of law enforcement and geographical locations.

A short man with a bull neck stood up. "Arnold Sanchez from F.B.I., Phoenix." He looked around, but the group was too tired to make the expected digs. It was either his wariness or the others' fatigue that might have raised the collective pressure they were under and which, in turn, suppressed any joking. Sanchez had piercing black eyes and spoke in a monotone. "If these people want to spread a virus, we think the best way to do so would be in a crowd."

A ranger from Dallas broke the rules and yelled out:

"Yeah, we feel likewise." Embarrassed, he sat down fast.

Flynn clucked. "Okay, guys, this ain't grade school. Yuh got somthin' ta say, jes' say it."

"Yeah," Stedmier said. "Let the ideas go. Didn' mean tuh inhibit you. We gotta git some answers, an' fast. So . . . *crowds?*"

Stone rose from his chair, towering over his superior, Guererro, sitting next to him. "That's the standard protocol we run into. Do the maximum damage by infecting the most. What they call a 'Super Spreader'"

"Right, sir." A young man in a suit, with not a hair out of place, stood up. "In Waco, anarchists threatened a toxic virus. We caught them trying to infiltrate a Baylor Bears' football game."

"So that's how you guys won the championship," came a call from a large group in the back.

Even Stedmier had to grin. The next minute his face was deadpan. "*Crowds.* Tha's a start."

Rogers, from Flynn's own unit, stood up. Shy and new, his face was flushed red. "I was thinking the 'West Texas Blowout'. Me an' the family were planning to go tomorrow. It's the last day and Rickey Lopez is going to be there."

An F.B.I. agent asked, "Who the hell's Rickey Lopez?"

"Who's Rickey Lopez?" It was asked by a freckle faced ranger who looked no more than sixteen. "You kiddin'?"

The F.B.I. man's eyes, tired as they appeared, flashed fire. "I'm from Colorado and I don't know who the guy is, and I don't care. I'm just trying to help you guys out and I don't need a lot of—"

Guerrero thrust from his chair. "*Agent Spencer!*"

Spencer sat down quickly. "Sorry, sir."

Stedmier jumped in. "Look guys, it's late an' eve'one is tired. You rangers, these out a' town agents ah helpin'out, so let's us show 'em some Texas hospitality."

The group quieted. Some of the rangers even made apologies to their neighbors.

"Aw' right," Stedmier said, "any other big gatherin's in town?"

"That's big doings for these parts," Rogers said. "We don't have too much going here in Midland." He laughed.

"You sure ain't kidding'," agreed his partner, sitting next to him.

"Okay." Flynn stood up. "Le's stop knocking our fair city. It pays your bills, yuh know. So, looks like we gonna put lots a resources over there. That damn Cimmarex Pavilion where it's gonna be, is huge. An' the land aroun'. Whoo boy." He looked at Guerrero. "We got maps an' aerial pitchus. Gonna need 'em. Would'n be surprised if they had two…three hun'red thousand fer the last day." He nodded to Rogers. "Git those pitchuhs, would yuh?"

Rogers returned with a stack of copies of Dalia's photograph. "This heah good-lookin' lady is the only one whose pitchuh we got," Flynn called above the appreciative whistles. "Cut th' shit, assholes!" He shook his head. "She's a damn terrorist, fer Chris sakes. There's anotha' non-A-rab, but we got no description a-tall fuh him." He tried to stifle a yawn, but couldn't help showing his yellowing teeth before continuing. "So tha's what we got. 'Fraid there ain't no more info, but you guys ah the best an' you'll protect this town, ah know. Nah le's git what sleep we kin, 'cause me, Stedmier an' your F.B.I. bosses ain' gonna be sleepin'. You all gonna be back 'roun' about five so git outta here an' git what rest yuh can." His eyes softened. "An' thanks, fellahs. We got a lot ridin' on this."

Stedmier's phone rang. "Hold on a minute, guys." As he listened, the creases in his bronzed face became more pronounced. "Thanks," he said quietly. For a moment, Stedmier just stared at his boots. His chest deflated with a long exhalation of breath. "Thet was our lab, gen'lmen. Accordin' ta them, this new covid tuh th' ol' one is like comparin' a Pop Warner football team ta the Unavu'sity a Texas varsity." Two fingers caressed the stubble on his chin. "Sa keep thet in mind and git back on time."

CHAPTER 22 COUNTDOWN

Kelly Frank sat sipping from her cup across from Senator Grossman's widow. The small apartment was filled with boxes and the shelves and walls were bare. Although the woman was cordial, she had never offered her first name. Kelly respected the distance. It was customary. The press was an intrusion.

"I returned just recently. And, I'm afraid, briefly." The pretty woman's eyes showed signs of grief that could not extinguish easily. "I'll be returning to our actual home near my parents. That's fine with me. As you can imagine, widows aren't encouraged to retain our housing once. . ." Her eyes clenched.

Kelly focused on her coffee as Mimi Grossman dabbed a tear. "Sorry," Mimi said it just above a whisper.

Kelly's expression registered the appropriate concern. Not that she didn't actually feel something, but certainly not to the degree that her tone indicated. *With what I've seen, I have to keep perspective,* she rationalized. "I certainly understand. Please don't apologize."

Mimi's hands fluttered in her lap. "Well, as I've told *everyone*, Arlo was not unhappy. We have a fine family-- and our relationship was better than most here in Washington—but, despite what the public thinks, the job has its pressures and he wasn't immune. In fact," her delicate eyebrows contracted over a slightly enlarged nose, "lately, he seemed more preoccupied than usual. He never told me why . . . he never did that. Didn't want me to worry."

Water welled up in her eyes once again. She dabbed it away, smiling. "I'm afraid that's all I can tell you." The lady stood up. Now her smile was very, very sad and she suddenly looked older. "Why would he kill himself? What wife ever knows her husband, no matter how much we may think we do? Politics is a secretive business. Unless you are a hard woman, you never hear all of it."

Kelly followed her to the door. The deceased senator's wife opened it and focused inward as she said, "I'm not one of those 'hard women.'" Mimi Grossman didn't say goodbye as she shut the door.

***

At 5:00 a.m. sharp, sleepy men, apprehensive about the day's potential for disaster, lined the corridors of the ranger headquarters. Coffee cups were filled repeatedly and the inadequate pile of morning sweets was soon depleted.

"While you guys were sleepin'," Stedmier quipped in front of the packed room, "we wuh workin'. Got yuh assignments right here on th' table. Lotta' you ah teamed up with strangers. Couldn' be helped. This ain't exactly a social get together. Map shows yuh all th' exits an' key places 'round the big stage. You'all got pitchures a' the woman an' those a' you covering parking lots got th' plates and description a the auto. We gonna be there long afore it opens, so yuh gonna see everyone comin' in, less they already there." His lips spread in a wicked grin. "An ah reckon you'all smart 'enough tuh figure out what to do if they ah there and shouldn' be."

Someone yelled out, "Like 'disappearing' them!" The

laughter was half-hearted partly due to the hour and partly because of the deadly nature of their task. Many of the younger ones, and barring only a few of the more experienced, had never been involved in anything of this magnitude. As one of the old pros put it to his team, "These mothers could take out an entire city and a good part of the damn country if we don't get them."

Flynn and Guerrero, standing next to Stedmier, also emphasized the extreme magnitude of the threat. As was usual, the F.B.I. agent wore a business suit and could have been attending a board meeting. "Just remember what that Covid did in 2020 and be double alert."

Flynn, sucking up his gut as much as possible, said, "Some a you boys remebuh losin' friends an' loved ones back then. Don' let it happen agin. Tha's all. God's speed ta each a yuh."

***

Felton and Croucher, from the Lubbock Rangers Office, drove into the huge open Cimarex Energy enclave. Groggy staff, forced to wake up early, grudgingly yanked open the large gates.

"Crazy sons of bitches." Croucher heard the words through his passenger window.

"You ain't kiddin'," he called back toward the shocked Mexican attendant. "We sure are."

His companion who was driving, said, "Worst thing about this, I gotta listen to hours of Mexican music. I hate Mexican music."

Croucher just laughed. "You Oklahomans don' know shit 'bout good music."

All surveillance was in place by 6:15. Rovers passed out coffee and exchanged quips, while Guerrero and Stedmier checked maps and repositioned personnel.

"Guess we're as ready as we're going to be," Guerrero said, as they sought out coffees.

Steadmier squinted up at the slowly ripening eastern sky. "Copters'u'll be here soon. Natural fuh them tuh be aroun' the Blowout. We gonna have advatisin' flyin' from 'em as a disguise."

Guerrero nodded. "Good thinking. And the medical teams will be on alert before nine. That's a mighty efficient little hospital they have here."

Stedmier added, "We beefed 'em up with specialists from Houston. They got a top-notch disease centuh out that way."

"I think we've covered as much as possible."

"Yeah," Stedmier agreed, as a young ranger brought coffee. "Here's hopin' it's enough ."

Guerrero took a gulp of coffee, wincing at the heat. "From your mouth to God's ear, Captain."

***

Sydney watched the early sunlight turn the room's gauzy curtain into molten gold. He stretched and then padded into the bathroom. Partially out of her sleep, Dalia cradled her head in one arm and blinked at the ceiling. When he returned, she rose and held out her arms. "A kiss for good luck."

Sydney accommodated, but the tension in his body was palpable as they hugged. She disengaged. "Your mind is not with me, love. I understand." She, too, made for the bathroom. For a moment he watched her, then, his disciplined mind ran through its check list. With the mental list concluded, Sydney reached for a Hetfield. *Running low,* he thought as he checked the pack. *Won't find these in Texas, that's certain. Well, soon as it's over, I'll be back in Europe. Just have to make do until . . . Only one thing more before we go. Plenty of time. Afternoon, early, should be the biggest crowd, listening to that country music. It's not bad, actually. Tells a lot of interesting stories.* He selected a pair of undershorts and began dressing.

They checked the room together, making sure nothing that might impart any information about them was left behind. Sydney flushed receipts and cigarette butts down the toilet, leaving nothing for the authorities, who would inevitably find the room. Any toiletries bearing fingerprints were taken with them. All surfaces were carefully wiped down with wet washcloths.

The virus was safely stored in reinforced vaporizer cans the size of small shaving cream dispensers. Each was gray, red and white. They made for appropriate celebratory accoutrements for the festive occasion at the Cimarex Energy Pavilion.

Sydney had explained the previous day how it was going to be done. "All we do is spray surfaces that people will touch. It lives on surfaces for up to a few days and in the air for a few hours. All we do is find a trash container; they're going to be all over the place. Lower one in deep and press the tab down. It locks like those insect foggers you've probably seen. Lower it deep. By the time it's spraying, we'll be gone. Just to be safe, we'll wear thin medical gloves. No one will notice since they're transparent, and in that mob, who's looking anyway? We will plant all eight, farthest first, and the last one no closer than five-hundred yards from our exit point to the car. Then we disappear. It's easy. They won't even know they're infected until we're on our flight out of here."

Dalia had shivered. "It's so easy, it's frightening."

"Yes," he agreed, his blue eyes expressionless. "As easy as killing gets."

They didn't check out. No need since his stolen card still had funds and, as many like it before, a dead or oblivious owner. The motel owner wouldn't learn that the card was stolen until long after their departure from Midland.

Early as it was, many autos filled the motel lot. Hidden behind a huge SUV, Sydney removed their license plate. "Let's take a walk." Around the corner, near the trash area, Sydney bent behind a red Toyota. "Keep an eye out, please." He deftly exchanged plates.

Driving away from the motel, Dalia asked, "Why change plates?"

Sydney surveyed nearby restaurants. "Think, my dear."

"They've had time to check with the car rentals at the airport."

"Precisely." He smiled, his teeth gleaming in the deepening sunlight. "You win an extra coffee."

"But they have no idea where we are," she persisted. "They think we're destroying oil operations, or their water supply."

"No bonus coffee for you. What is my first rule: Why

take chances?"

Although her nerves were on edge, the dark-haired girl mustered a smile. "You do think of everything, my dear." His almost heroic face was only marred by a rather weak chin. Still, to Dalia, Sydney was as godlike as Zeus. His answer was sharp and confident. "To survive in this business, you must. Forget that and you're dead. Please remember that, if nothing else."

Denny's restaurant was on the right. Sydney turned in. "We'll drive to the back, so I can put on the new plate. Then a hearty breakfast." He patted Dalia's knee. "We have a long day ahead. I want us to be at Dallas/Fort Worth International later tonight for the first flight going east or, better yet, to Europe."

As they entered, Sydney fondled her rear. "I've recanted. You still may have your bonus coffee."

CHAPTER 23 ORANGE SOMBRERO

Croucher slid off his Stetson, wiping perspiration from his freckled forehead with the back of his wrist. He let his gaze roam over the lines of automobiles in the Pavilion's large parking area. "Sheet, Felton, we been watchin' that gate fer hours. I've seen enough dang Hondas to be countin' 'em in my sleep from now till Christmas. An' we didn' see no license plate like we're lookin' for."

"You ain't kiddin'," said his taller companion. "A'fore I was a Ranger, I wrangled cattle and I gotta tell you, it couldn't'a been any hotter than this damn parkin' lot. But we gotta keep checkin' lest the car got in without nobody seein' it."

They started down another row. "Hondas. Hondas. Ever'body's got fuckin' Hondas. An' white more'n anything," griped Croucher. "Why couldn' the assholes have a Volvo. Nobody down here drives those."

Croucher adjusted his hat. "Yeah. That'd be good." Puffing out air from beneath his trim mustache, he took the opposite side of the row from his partner.

As the two continued to scan the license plates on both sides of the present row, an ocean of additional vehicles continued to form new rows to their right.

***

Flynn cursed the heat, but Stedmier knew it was really the pressure. Stedmier yelled to be heard above the nearby entertainment. "Yep, ah feel the same, Toby. So damn many people, an' this place is as big a damn exhibition groun' as we got. Holds country fairs, conventions, livestock shows, eva'thing big."

"Ain't no Dallas," said Flynn, "but fer us, this is thee center a the world. The F.B.I. got ana'thing?"

The band kicked into a fast tempo and Stedmier had to yell even louder. He cupped his hands around his mouth. "Not so far, Toby."

Rivulets of sweat trickled down Flynn's round cheeks as he observed a group of scrubby haired youths in shirts with filthy slogans. They were merrily passing around reefers and moved spastically — completely out of sync with the Latin beat. Flynn signaled with his head and moved in their direction.

"He's jus' doin' that ta be doin' something, thought Stedmier. *Ain't no way those chactuhs gonna destroy a thing but their own brains.*

***

An attendant waved Sydney and Dalia on toward a row so long its terminus blurred in the hazy summer air. Eventually, vacant spots materialized and Sydney nosed their vehicle into one. Immediately, an enormous RV pulled up next to them, releasing a swarm of celebrating Mexicans with gaudy sombreros the size of small tires. Their powerful car speakers blasted mariachi music for all to hear. One happy occupant offered Sydney tequila, which he calmly declined. The rotund man shrugged and wandered after his departing friends.

"If they're all like that, we're in good shape," remarked Sydney. "Let's join the fun." He tugged on a ten-gallon he had purchased at a store outside the fairgrounds. "How do I look?"

Dalia giggled. "Like Cactus Pete." She donned an orange sombrero with bright yellow tassels, which until then she had kept at her side. "And I?"

"Beautiful in anything." Then he frowned. "But how did you sneak that past me? I told you conservative. We don't want attention."

"Thank you, gallant sir, and it's a woman's prerogative what she wears." She smiled coquettishly. "Don't you know that?" She touched his cheek. "I grabbed it from a stand we passed. C'mon now. It made me happy and soothed my nerves. What's wrong with that?"

Still angry, Sydney was about to say more but thought better of it. *She is nervous enough without my getting on her case.* He said, "Well, we *are* here at a festival … so why not?" He laughed. But the dead blue in his eyes belied his lighthearted response.

"Yes, we are." She struggled to smile through his unspoken rebuke. Then her dark eyes clouded. "In a manner of speaking," she said quietly.

Deep understanding radiated from his eyes. Then, the curtain went down. In its place, only fathomless mist. He gripped the woman's hand so hard that she nearly gasped. "We have a job. We'll do it. Some will suffer . . . many won't." The door handle *snapped* closed in his hand. "Let's go." Sydney was already surrounded by revelers as she followed.

***

F.B.I. agent Rolph Taggs, from Colorado, hated the heat. He also wasn't very fond of Latinos or their music, having come from a high school where every day was a battle to escape roving Mexicans seeking out "white boys" to trash. Now he sweated profusely as he sorted his way through a Spanish-speaking ocean of bodies. A crumpled Xerox copy of the wanted girl's face was clutched in his hand. *Sheet. I get volunteered for this bullshit assignment in the middle of summer . . . and I don't even give a shit if half these Mexicans get blown up in the first place. We got plenty of oil shale in other states, if it comes to that.*

A pretty little family of three blonde girls, chattering away to beat the band, passed within a few feet. Taggs sighed, almost muttering aloud to himself. *Quit your griping. There's a lot of good people here—including Latinos—that don't deserve to die from a disease just for living near oil. And, oil is important if Russia and China and the rest of our enemies put the screws to us. So get on with the job, Taggs.* He studied the throng. *Hats and more hats. How can I see their faces beneath those huge sombreros? Gee.*

A little way ahead of Taggs, a raucous band of white youths bumped into a woman, sending her brightly colored sombrero flying. Her tall companion roughly scattered the boys as he hurried to retrieve it.

One of the group objected and was met with a highly effective knuckle fist to the solar plexus. It stopped him dead. He wilted in slow motion, his body falling beneath the feet of the crowd. Surging pedestrians sprawled over him and a buildup of bodies ensued. Screaming bystanders waved unsuspecting revelers away. Others reached down to aid the squirming victims.

Suspicious of the tall man's unusually effective violence, the F.B.I. agent scrutinized the scene, searching for a lovely face he had recognized from the picture in his hand. She was no longer there. He thrust his way through the milling bodies, breaking out on the other side, running for all he was worth toward that bright orange sombrero which her violent companion had slapped back upon her head. As he scurried past an ice cream booth, only feet from his quarry, the man turned and something punched Taggs' gut. It seemed so light that the agent hardly noticed. Yet three steps later his entire abdomen was on fire. He looked down. His white shirt was as red as the costumes of a nearby group of mariachis. His numbing legs no longer held his weight. Taggs sprawled into the mariachis, ruining the finale of their specialty: *Guadalajara.*

After thrusting the gory knife into a loaded receptacle, Sydney hurried to catch up with Dalia. "It appears that they are on to you, my dear." He grabbed her arm, hustling her toward a row of Porta Potties. They scurried behind the long row.

"What happened?" asked Dalia. "What's the matter?"

Sydney looked full into her face. His eyes were blue slivers. "Someone knew you, my dear." His voice was unperturbed but his eyes flashed blue fire. "How could that be?"

"I . . . I don't have any idea. Who could?"

Sydney asked calmly. "Did you spread the virus?"

Dalia was suddenly frightened of the man she thought was her lover. "Not so much, but some. We didn't have much time—"

"Yes, yes, I know. I also did some . . . but not as much as I planned."

She pushed back the sombrero which his rough treatment had forced too far forward. He ripped it from her head. The string that held it wrenched her neck.

"Whaa!"

He yelled, *"That's a red flag, dammit. I told you. Anybody would recognize that, now. How could I be so stupid to let you keep it?"*

"But it was so unique," Dalia protested.

"Unique is what fucks you!" Cocking his wrist, he flung it, Frisbee-like. It landed on a tall bush eight feet above the ground. Narrow branches swayed under its weight. It sat there bobbing like a bright kite.

"Hey, that orange sombrero." A voice came from their right. "The dying guy said that he was chasing it."

Two figures in complete black uniforms separated themselves from the passing crowd. They stared upward. Both officers left the path for a closer look, their eyes riveted on the hat. Suddenly they noticed the man and woman near the end of the front row of toilets. Tense hands scrabbled at holsters. Much too late.

Sydney leveled his Heckler and Koch, taking the first in the eye and his companion in the throat. Although the shots were not silenced, the crowd and music dimmed the effect of the sharp *cracks*.

"Around to the back," he yelled to Dalia. "Hurry."

Dalia scampered after him to the far end of the second row of toilets. Then around to the front. None were in use so far back.

He faced her. Her own Glock trembled in her hand. Dalia's eyes never stopped scanning side to side. She fought to control her voice but it quavered anyway. "What do we do, Sydney?"

A sad smile crossed his face. "They know who you are." He sighed. "I don't know how . . . but they do. My guess is that the country that hired me, and their partners, got cold feet. They're cutting their losses and pressured Hezbollah to turn over your picture to U.S law enforcement." His shoulders tensed. "It's always the way with these cowards when the going gets rough." Sydney's lips curled. "And they leave us holding the bag because we are disposable."

"But we committed . . . everything." Dalia stared up at him, her dark eyes searching for an answer. "Everything," she repeated like a confused child.

For the second time in as many minutes, the icy blue slivers appeared in his eyes. "Sorry, my dear. No matter how important we think we are; no matter what they make us believe . . . the bastards will always fuck us. *Damn their souls*." He spat. "And damn them for what they make me do."

Dalia blinked at the man she had come to love. His face, his breathing. Although he was outwardly calm, she suddenly saw Sydney as a wild animal trapped in its lair. *What is going through his mind?* she wondered. She knew she could be a tiger to his lion and more than anything they needed to complete the mission, live or die. *Get it together girl,* she told herself as she skulked before the toilets. The muscle between Sydney's right thumb and index finger caught Dalia square in the neck and the taut web between his fingers began to crush her larynx. Her eyes bulged. The moments that she had known Sydney intimately flashed before her eyes, like the memory of a lost and barely believable dream . Then—no consciousness. Then nothing.

He gripped the *gurgling* girl under her arms as he eased open the plastic door of a toilet. Her sightless eyes, trapped in a frozen expression of shock, were the last memory Sydney would ever have of her. He laid her gently on the bench next to its odoriferous opening in the plastic floor. Her hair dangled into its dark hollow. If there was regret, no sign of it reflected in his features. Sydney murmured something unintelligible and shut her corpse into the darkness.

The noise of the crowd gathered around the dead policemen dimmed as Sydney made off into the bushes. Ahead, the giant speakers of the main bandstand throbbed with deafening beats. He calmly walked toward them.

***

"Two cops shot over in this area." Stedmier pointed out a section of the map to the right of the bandstand. "Let's git, Toby."

Both Rangers rushed toward the section, pushing past revelers singing along with the entertainer on stage. Most separated reluctantly, despite the uniforms, angry that their swinging in time to the Latin beat was being interrupted. The path led to the food stands and rows of toilets. Overhead, the orange sombrero fluttered innocently above the carnage it had caused.

"Sheez," said Flynn, "two shots, two deaths. Whoever

they ah, they got purty good aim."

Stedmier was familiar with Flynn's often frivolous commentaries upon death, knowing that it was his friend's defense against the horrors that he had witnessed in his long career. *We all develop our coping strategies*, he thought. *Otherwise, who could do the job for long?*

A police sergeant with deep lines at the corners of eyes that had seen too much, strode over. "Nobody saw the perps," he said, anticipating the Rangers' first question. "All too busy trying to help . . . 'course, 'help' was a moot point for these poor men by that time. Understand one of your guys was killed back there." He signaled behind him with a thumb.

Stedmier said, "Actu'lly, F.B.I., but yeah." He was anxious to pursue his own questions. "Did they radio in anythin' before?"

"Yeah," the man nodded. "That orange thing up there." He pointed at the sombrero. As if on cue, it spiraled to the ground. "We all heard that it was picked up by a blond tall guy and given to the girl who's in the photo you handed out. Your guy—or F.B.I.—mentioned it as he died. That's what..." He stopped, clenching his jaw. "Lucas and Steve . . ."

"Yeah, I get it, sergeant."

The officer continued as if he hadn't heard. "Their weapons weren't even drawn. No one heard the shots with the crowd noise and music . . . didn't even have a chance. No one saw a thing."

Flynn's eyes went to the row of toilets. "Yuh, think?"

Steadmier's eyes met his friend's. "Lots of bushes past

the row. They didn't have much time." He shrugged, drawing his revolver. "Worth a try. I've heard a stranguh things." It took them all of five minutes, knocking on doors to allow innocents to vacate, before the Rangers and policeman got to the end and turned into the back row. Stedmier pulled open the last door. "Well, holy shit."

They dragged the girl out, laying her upon a grassy patch.

Flynn bent with difficulty. "Look at thet purple throat an' thet expression. Girl sure wasn't expectin' to end up dead in a shitter."

"Yeah," said the cop. "When you play with matches . . ." He continued to stare at the body. "Bitch is even prettier than her picture."

Flynn looked up. "Not a damn thing on her, 'cept that Glock in there. Ain't been fired. And these." He gingerly shook her pocket. Two metal spray bottles rolled out. They were colored bright red and white.

All three men stared at the bright little containers. "Is that what I think it is," asked the wide-eyed policeman, stepping further back. "Is that why we had an alert for those two? No one told us the exact reason."

Stedmier said, "We sure think so. Our medical team will be ovuh in a few minutes. Don't let no one neah that toxic shit."

"Don't worry." The sergeant squinted toward the bushes. "My guess is he went through there to mix in with the concert—if you could call it that." His eyes teared. "Please get the bastard—"

"You bet we will," Stedmier said, patting the man's

shoulder. "Thanks for the help. Stay with your boys. We'll call in our teams, now. We'll get our guys ovuh to take her an' the rest a' the evidence, if it's all raht?"

The tearful sergeant said, "Sure. Whatever you say, Ranger. Since it's in our jurisdiction, just let us know you got the--"

"Of course we will," Stedmier reassured him. Suddenly he stopped. "One more thing. Think you could help mah people round-up some of those who saw the man she was with?"

The sergeant shook his head, shrugging. "They were all pretty vague but we got some names and they all said they'd be around for the wrap up at four. We'll do our best."

"Can our guys contact you, Sergeant—"

"Raymer, with an 'm'. I'll be waiting near *my boys.*" He nodded in the direction of the fallen police officers.

Stedmier raised sympathetic hands. "Sure. C'mon, Toby. Let's ketch that concert. Call in some a' the boys tuh meet us. Send two more over there with that sergeant. Also, let Guererro know 'bout his fallen man, in case he don't already. See if some a' them kin meet up with us at the bandstand."

***

The Master of Ceremonies was a tiny speck on the huge stage, but his voice rumbled through the massive speakers set at intervals throughout the crowd. "And now, one of your favorites: Ruben Ramos and the Mexican Revolution."

The audience exploded as Sydney worked his way back

toward the crowd's outer fringe and the parking lots. Wildly cheering spectators made the passing difficult, but he deftly butted back without incident. As he broke free, a brightly clad group of musicians in front of a cluster of tall bushes caught his eye. Without hesitation, he angled toward them, disappearing into the foliage behind.

"Hey, Juanito, you gotta piss again," a voice called out. "Do eet back there."

"I already did, estupido. Thee fucking toilets was too far and our man goes on next. We gotta get movin' soon as I fineesh weeth my leettle inspiration here."

From the sweet aroma blowing toward him, Sydney had no doubt what the 'inspiration' was.

"Yeah, Juanito," called a different voice. "You couldn't find a note on that geetar without your weed."

"Marico'n," Juanito answered. "I can find any note before you cahn fin' your pinga chiquita." This brought a laugh from the others.

The other responded, "Besa mi culo, Juanito!" This brought another laugh.

"Changa tu madre," Juanito yelled. He separated from the bushes near Sydney.

The man was small and round, singing and humming as he sought out his friends. His dark eyes went wide at the sight of the tall man. His mouth opened, but before Juanito could scream, Sydney's spread knuckles reached his solar plexus and stifled any sound. A thumb thrust to his fleshy throat finished him.

Sydney caught the body before it could tumble to the ground. Apparently, death released the bladder's surplus content, which dripped down the Mexican's legs. Carefully laying Juanito down away from his mess, Sydney stripped the dead man of his black cape and massive sombrero. It was black with gold trim and dangling gold tassels. The rest of the apparel was too small and starting to smell.

Slipping off the large guitar from the mariachi's side, Sydney was careful not to touch the strings. *Music is undesirable at this point,* he thought, *as if I could play, anyway. No point in hiding the body . . . and no time.*

With the guitar in hand, the tall man circled the bushes behind his victim's chattering companions, who started to call the dead man's name repeatedly. Sydney emerged among the parked cars a hundred feet away.

Above, two helicopters *throbbed* in the pure blue sky. Banners advertising the event below wriggled in the high breezes.

Sydney squinted upward. *Should have expected that.*

At least two more now *throbbed* overhead. *Bugger those copters. Too many . . . and only two trailing advertising. They're looking for me!* Sydney stopped, protected from the sky by his sombrero. *They must have known in advance that the attack was biological. Then it would have been easy for them to deduce that these crowds would be the target, not empty oil wells. Otherwise, how could they have so many whirlybirds circling so soon?*

His hands clenched. *When this is over, I* will *find out who the leaker is . . . goddamn politicians hire me, then panic*—The icy slivers appeared in his eyes. *When I find out . . . even if it's Hezbollah . . .* Sydney shook off the thoughts. *No time now. Relax. There's hundreds of white*

Hondas like my rental on the grounds, at least. And I changed the plates.

Wrapped in his cape, and with his massive sombrero shielding him from above, Sydney proceeded confidently toward his car. Although little children snuck peeks at the tall entertainer, no one questioned his departure, despite the fact that the grand finale was less than an hour off.

***

Flynn's walkie-talkie squawked. "A dead mariachi on the far side a the main audience," Flynn told Stedmier. "Mus' be our boy done it."

"Makin' fer his car's, my guess. He musta' had enough. Tell the helicopt'ahs. Gotta be in one a'hem white Hondas. Let's see if he's leaving early, Toby."

Flynn's forehead crushed down on his fleshy nose. "Yeah, oughta be a coupla' thousan' of those little Jap cahs. Buy American ah always say. Guerrero's coordinatin' it. Ah'll contact him."

After Flynn's brief conversation, Steadmier's walkie-talkie popped on again. "Couldn't get my superior, sir, so I used your frequency. Hope that's okay."

"Sure, wha's up?"

"Well, we talked to that group of musicians—guess they're mariachis—and the dead gentleman was missing his sombrero and cape. Thought that might be important."

Eyes wide, Steadmier said, "Sure is, Ranger. Sure is. What colors? . . . Mostly black cape, gold trim an' black sombrero with gold tassels. Good work." He shoved Flynn, who was still talking. "Toby." He pushed his friend a second time.

"Okay, okay, gotta git off," Flynn said. His thick nose wrinkled. "What the fuck, Sted?"

"Our guy stole a Mex hat an' cape." He repeated the description to Flynn. "Git it out!"

Flynn barked the description out on all channels. "That'll help. People gonna notice a Mariachi outfit, fuh sure, 'specially a guy that tall an' leavin' early like that."

"Sho' hope so. Le's hustle ta that gate. Think yuh can make it, Toby?"

"I'll beat yo' sorry ass," Flynn said and broke into a tottering run.

"Jus' don' go given yusself a heart attack, ol' timer." Stedmier laughed as he commenced a slow trot.

Pumping hard, Flynn sent a bird Stedmier's way. "I'll be there waitin' fo' yuh, sonny boy. Don' yuh worry."

CHAPTER 24 WHITE HONDA

A passing crowd of teenage revelers adopted Sydney. All were Mexican, making up a group of maybe thirteen to sixteen. They bought into his story of getting his guitar strings from his car, in case he broke one during his performance. His Spanish was excellent, as were his French, German and Russian, and to a lesser degree, Italian and Greek. And, of course, Afrikaans. Together, the youngsters formed an innocent escort; just an adult escorting his kids and their friends.

When his recent admirers asked him to play for them, Sydney begged off. He hugged two of the kids before striding rapidly toward his Honda. Pressing the starter, he carefully backed out. *An accident now is all I'd need.*

His wide hat hit the visor. *"Bloody hell!"* he cursed. Sydney was about to toss it when he thought better of it. *Might be handy for checking at the gates. Also the cape. Better than anyone seeing my face. Who knows if they already have my description from those seeing that bloody orange hat of Dalia's?*

Slowly following the departing vehicles toward the gate, he loosened his body, adopting the giddy attitude of a fan as he turned the radio to a Latin music station and kicked up the volume.

***

Two weeks before, Manuel Rodriguez, and his family, parents, aunts, uncles and cousins— all dressed up so nice—had had a proud day as the star of a Texas Ranger was pinned upon his chest. Now the newly appointed Ranger diligently checked outgoing cars at the main gate. He'd been made aware that the local rangers, as well as the F.B.I., were on the lookout for a tall Caucasian in a white Honda. However, word had not reached him yet with the intel about Sydney's Mariachi apparel.

As the white Honda rolled up, Manuel's right hand lowered to his holster. His breath quickened. Then he heard the car radio blasting his favorite song by Vicente Fernandez, and the young ranger relaxed. The huge sombrero, tottering above a head apparently feeling no pain, caused him to smile. "Hey, amigo, you okay to drive?"

"Shurr. No am emboracho. Jus' haffing good time, Mr. Ran-gah. Jou know how eet ees. I be fine. Sure, I be muy bueno."

Straight out of training, the young recruit followed the book. "I just want to make sure, sir, for yours, and everyone else's' safety. Could you remove your hat?"

"Please, I okay."

"Your hat please, sir."

Just then, Manuel's radio crackled. "A moment, sir. I'll be right with you." He walked away to listen. Returning, the young ranger's hand returned to his revolver more purposefully. "Just a moment, sir. Your hat—"

The big sombrero filled nearly the entire driver's window. As Manuel drew his weapon, a shot from behind the huge hat exploded against his chest. His revolver dropped out of frozen fingers as he back pedaled three steps, sinking to his knees.

His partner, busy with the double line of departing vehicles, rushed to the stricken man. It was too late. Cursing, he grabbed for his own weapon. But by then, the Honda was lost in exiting traffic.

After checking Rodriguez's pulse, teary-eyed Tylan Moore called in. "My partner's dead. Shot by your suspect . . . Manny's dead. He didn't have a chance . . . please get the bastard . . . sorry . . . okay, he's heading toward either 191 or 250 . . . could go either way. Fuck . . . sorry. So much blood."

"Steady, son, steady," Flynn spoke back into his walkie-talkie. "Gotta keep yuh head. Yuh say either a those roads . . . okay. We'll git men on it. Stay with your pahtner till we git help. Yuh did a good job, rookie."

Immediately, Flynn clicked on his radio, blinking away perspiration and ignoring Stedmier's raised eyebrows. "All cahs head toward entrances to 191 and 250. Suspect's white Honda attemptin' entry. He jus' killed a Ranger . . . ah repeat, Ranger down . . . Ranger coptah and po-lice coptahs head fer those exits from the complex. Follah suspect vehicle and inform us a' progress. The rest a you, try tuh stop thet sombitch . . . but careful a' civilians. We'll be headin' yuh way. Keep yuh radios on."

Their empty vehicle was two hundred feet ahead at the main gate observation point. "We gonna git that duhty son of a bitch." Flynn puffed and gasped as they scrambled toward it.

"Yuh damn well know we will," Stedmier growled. "An' don' be afraid tuh kill him, neithuh."

***

Always have an exit strategy, Sydney told himself. Swinging the wheel before the exits to either 250 or 191, he took a sharp left at Deauville Boulevard. It was a street skirting a residential area close to the grounds where the *Blowout* was wrapping up. All the vehicles surrounding his Honda continued on toward the entrances to the highways a quarter of a mile ahead.

Sydney glanced back at the queue he had departed. Bunched vehicles slowly nudged their way onto their respective ramps, causing a massive jam accompanied by cacophonous horns and screeching brakes. *Heavy traffic . . . may not have noticed me slip out of line as they set up a chase. Here's hoping—.*

On the side road, he passed a series of industrial buildings and skeletal parking structures. Being Sunday, everything was closed. Sydney toyed with the idea of driving into one of the vacant five-story garages and waiting out the pursuit. He quickly dismissed the thought. *If they catch me in there, I'll have nowhere to run.* Soon the homes of Grassland Estates, modern and sprawling, were on his right. His preconceived plan was to turn into the acres and acres of flat scrubby land across from Grasslands and wait, unobserved.

All at once, a rapid *thumping* permeated the air above. *Bloody helicopters. I should have guessed. Cars might never have found me but whirlybirds . . .* Sydney's eyes were intent. A quarter mile farther on the left was an insignificant sign perched on a rickety wooden post. It was bent from storms like a frail oldster.

There! exulted Sydney, throwing the Honda onto a

chalky white trail the width of a car. *This empty land is full of these white roads. Don't know where they go but this has got to work. Knew about these from good old Google Earth—but, then, I always take the extra step, don't I?*

Clouds of chalky material, comprised of alkaline soil and random minerals in powdered form, rose alongside Sydney's speeding vehicle. Squinting through the gyrating particles, the tall man rotated his head right to left and back as he fought the wheel of the sliding vehicle. *Hope this dust blinds that chopper while I find just what I'm looking for or*—he gritted his teeth. *Don't worry, old man, they haven't got you yet.*

Before him, miles upon miles of twisted trees thrust out of crusted earth. Patches of yellowing grass, splayed like the hair on a nervous cat's back, dotted the landscape. Random rocks, ranging from the size of baseballs to boulders, littered the ground. The parched earth wore splotches of white mineral matter, like pieces of tattered wedding gowns. Everywhere, frantic crawlies scurried away from the car in swivel-jointed panic.

Suddenly, Sydney's lips spread in a grim smile. *Yes, that should do it.* The Honda bumped and *clattered* over rocks and cement-hard earth toward a rocky outcropping. Without hesitation, he swerved into a formidable bolder. Its shadowy crevices protruded tusk-like, peeling the front half of his hood clear back to the windshield. Ducking low, he avoided the shower of glass that sprayed the interior. Steam from the crushed radiator billowed into the air, wreathing the vehicle in a vaporous shroud. Under this misty cover, Sydney crawled back drunkenly toward the trunk. He *clicked* it open and sprawled, headfirst. As the cloud dissipated, he lay half in and half out, legs dangling. The copter's shadow hovered over Sydney's stationary body.

***

Ranger Pearson Edwards and his pilot, Ranger J.B. Smith, flew above the entries to the two main departure routes from the concert. They had just received the news of their dead comrade at the gate.

"Thet sumbitch," said Smith. "Ah hope we' the ones who ketch his ass. Sumbitch."

Edwards opened the foil on a Juicy Fruit pack. "Well, with this mob pouring out we're gonna have the devil's own time sorting out a white Honda from that herd."

Smith adjusted the rotor. "Tha's why they pay us th' big bucks, padnuh.

"Sheet, do you see what I see? A damn white Honda and look." Edwards jabbed his index finger right, multiple times. "It's veering off down Deauville and going too fast to be turning into that group of houses."

Smith stared out of the Plexiglas bubble. "You' right. It's Sunday, so he ain't going tuh them commercial buidin's or parking garages . . . mebbe he's headin' fo' the Grasslands. There's plenty a' houses ovah there."

"Bank her right, Smitty," Edwards said, "and let's see. We can fly back before the main if it's a false alarm. I'll radio the police chopper to keep an eye out." With intense *throbbing*, the copter banked right. Edwards hunched forward, staring down at their quarry. His uneaten gum remained pinched between his fingers. "Can't believe he was thinking of going into those garages, Smitty. Guy can't be a local even thinking of doing that. He sure doesn't live around here—whoa, there he goes, see? He's haul-assing his way past Grasslands. Stay close. Sheet, he's turning into nowheres-ville. Must have heard us." Edwards stuck the gum between his lips. "He's our guy, Smitty—he's our guy for sure!"

The helicopter wobbled as a torrent of white particles spattered against their rotor. "Bettuh elevate," said Smith. "Cain't see through thet shit an' it sure ain't no good fer my Bessie, here." He patted the copter's canopy.

At the higher elevation, their view cleared. "Wow, he went an' hit that fuckin' rock head-on. Look'it that guy, wobbly an' all, Pearce—" Smith dipped the copter for a closer look. "He sure musta' taken a wallop in the noggin—fuck if'n he don' look like ah did aftuh yo' bachelor pahty. An' he's got thet damn cape on—he's sure enough our guy!"

Pearson was already unbuckling. "Let's get down there and snag the bastard. He doesn't look like he'll be much trouble. I'll radio the location, best as I can. Little sign about a quarter mile past Greenland Estates on the left with a big dirt entry, wouldn't you say?"

Smith banked right. "Yeah, that'll git it. Lot of our boys know this area." They straightened. Then Smith swayed the copter seventy feet above the wreck. Steam from the radiator spurted from both sides, funneling upward into the hot air. Smith squinted down at the distressed vehicle. "Don' forget, he killed one a' ours. Le's not be too nice. Keep yuh Colt readuh when we go in . . . no tellin'."

Edwards unsnapped the safety on his DSG Alpha

Holster, a Ranger favorite.

***

"Sounds like they got 'em. Le's fly," said Flynn. He grabbed the radio. "All a you git the hell off those highways an' come on back tuh 158. The bastud's going off on one 'a them little white roads right aftuh the Grasslands. There's a little broken sign there, as ah recall . . . but no matter. It's a mighty big dirt turn-out. You locals know the way, so he'p yuh pardners. Honda's wrecked 'bout a quarter mile down. Our copter's theh. Cain't miss it. Now git!"

Stedmier backed up fast, *screeching* the wheels right as he flashed on the light bar and nudged his way into the traffic. Slamming his horn repeatedly, he cursed at confused drivers who literally had nowhere to go. He *slammed t*he dash, knocking his Stetson into Flynn's lap.

"We'll be out soon," Flynn said in a consoling voice. "Ain't nothin' for it, Sted."

***

With the chopper still fifty feet up, Sydney carefully screwed the propelling charge into the end of the RPG-7 warhead stored in the trunk. *Glad we grabbed this bad boy back in Laredo,* he thought. *You just never know, do you?* Once done, he loaded the pointed warhead onto the launcher, lining it up with the trigger mechanism. *Tough keeping my legs dangling loose while I do this, but if they think I'm functioning, they could take off.* He figured the cape should hide any other movement they might see and planned to leave it and the sombrero inside the car, thinking that should be helpful in establishing his demise. *At least temporarily*, he had the very gall to pray—*that should be all I'll need.*

The fact that he invoked God's help held no irony for Sydney. "I've seen God's help in action and he is none too selective," he'd once explained to a priest during the bloody Rhodesian conflict. "I have as much a right to ask for it as anybody."

When his ears told him that the helicopter was descending further, Sydney eased the weapon toward the left side of his body. *I really don't have to move fast. Where are those poor bastards going to go? Just a little closer, friends . . .*

***

"I thought I saw his legs move a little, Smitty. Think we should wait? He can't get anywhere without us seeing."

Smith wrinkled his longish nose. "Ah didn' see nothin' like thet. Lots a currents what with th' hot air . . . n' all. Tell yuh, ah'd sure like ta be standin' there with mah big Colt out when the otha's come a stormin' up. Now wouldn' thet be cool, Pearce-boy?"

Edwards grinned, revealing a Kirk Douglas-sized dimple. "Yeah. 'Hero Rookies,' the papers might say. Okay, *let's do it!*"

They were twenty feet and slightly to the right when Sydney sprang out of the trunk with the lethal tube resting on his shoulder. His head tilted into the sight. At its end was a spear-like device similar to the head of a harpoon.

Pearce screamed, "Pull up. Pull up, now! *That's a damn RPG7.* I saw one at my reserve meeting one time. Holy

Mother, evade if you can! *It'll cremate us! Go, Smith. Go, for Chirssakes!*

Frantically grabbing at the controls, Smith overcompensated, sending the helicopter into a spin. Before his sweating fingers could regain control his partner screamed, *"Oh shit!"* Then their bubble was in flames. Pure heat scalded the pilot's face. His eyes went sightless.

Edward's pain-filled howls blended with the *crackling of the* polycarbonate canopy.

As the copter spun faster and faster and the heat consumed his body, Ranger J.B. Smith mercifully lapsed into unconsciousness . . . forever.

***

Dropping the deadly tube, Sydney lunged as far from his car as possible. As he scurried behind a small rock outcropping, he covered his head with his arms before the concussion and heat caught up with him. Cowering behind his pitifully inadequate barrier, Sydney dug his face into the pliant mixture of sand and soil beneath his face, praying that flaming pieces of the bucking copter wouldn't slice him up. He remained down as the dying aircraft—much closer and infinitely louder—crushed what was left of the Honda. Seconds later, the detonation of the car's erupting gas tank drowned out the *crackling* of the dying aircraft.

Eventually, the heat dissipated and the tall man peeked around his rocky wall, patting its rough top. "You weren't big, but you did the job. Whoa . . ." He ducked as a molten piece of metal—burned past recognition—*whooshed* by, just inches over his head. After that, Sydney stayed glued to his rocks for many minutes. Eventually he dusted off and tentatively rose a second time.

The helicopter and Honda had fused into a smoldering heap like obliterated robots in a space war movie. Eruptions of flame spurted, and smoke hung heavy over the carnage, floating listlessly in the heat. Flames randomly spurted as the searching fire located fresh material within the molten structure.

Rising cautiously, Sydney observed the carnage. It resembled the red-hot fusion of destroyed flying saucers in *War of the Worlds*. Satisfied, he moved closer, yanking off his cape. It was soiled but undamaged. He flung it upon the portion that originally had been his vehicle. *Just a little more proof, besides the Sombrero. It should be enough to leave them guessing. That's all I need . . . a little time.*

If there were bodies in the surreal shape of the copter, Sydney couldn't possibly tell. The only recognizable part was one perfectly preserved tire thrown free of the conflagration. Still, the tall man faced what he assumed was the cockpit. "I salute you, honored warriors. God guide you home," he said aloud without irony.

For a moment, Sydney squinted at the sky beyond the smoke. It showed bright and blue, indifferent to the tragedy below.

No throbbing companions of the downed copter filled the air. No telltale chalky plumes of approaching vehicles ruffled the roads. Satisfied, Sydney broke into a fast trot, proceeding deeper into the desolate acreage.

***

"Fuck, what'a mess." Flynn stared teary eyed at the ruins. "Could see th' damn smoke clear back tuh the pahkin' lot. Two of mah rookies . . . what am I my 'sposed to tell their mommas?"

Stedmier stood silent.

The heavy ranger wiped an eye with the back of his wrist, "Gee, it's near impossible ta tell where the coptah ends an' th' Honda begins."

Law enforcement from four other flashing vehicles silently stared. Each nursed his own thoughts.

Stedmier strode fifteen feet away, lifting a smoldering piece of cloth. "Scrap a' his cape," he said, passionlessly. "And..." Stedmier rushed to a blackened tube propped against a rock. "Well, ah'll be."

"What, Sted?"

"Still too hot, but less'n ah miss my guess, part of a goddamn grenade launcha'. These boys did'n have th' chance of a snowball in hell."

Flynn stared at the object through red-rimmed eyes. "I hope the bastud fried slow." He spat at the glowing rubble.

Steadmier's leather face was impassive. "Le's git th' right people to sort this out . . . an' copters to search a coupl'a miles in each di-rection."

Flynn's eyebrows rose. "Yuh don' thaink—"

An unpleasant vision prodded Stedmier's brain but all he said was, "Nah, but let's check ana'way."

Flynn shook his head, looking down at his dusty shoes and kicking up a pile of small stones as he went for his car radio. "You the boss, but—"

"*Toby*—" Steadmier interrupted, "ah jus' don' trust this devil tuh die. Don' know why . . . spooky intuition mebbe, *but ah jus' don'tI*"

CHAPTER 25 THE GREAT ESCAPE

His sprint had moderated to a jog and, finally, a fast walk. *Sweating my ass off*, thought Sydney, raking his fingers through extremely damp hair. Turning back, he squinted toward where he had last seen the column of smoke from the wrecks. It appeared insignificant in the far distance.

He blinked away perspiration enveloping his eyes, thinking, *Bloody lucky they don't send out those birds. Guess they bought my demise. An hour more and I'll turn east toward that community I passed.*

Almost immediately there was *throbbing* in the distance. He looked up. *What do you know, I, spoke too soon. From this distance looks like those bloodhounds have three helicopters. Thorough, aren't they? Well, I am prepared for that, too.*

Sydney sought out a tangle of brush between two scrubby trees about eighty feet away. *That ought to do.* Once there, he kicked at the soil. *Nice and soft. Good.* Dropping to his knees, he scooped away large portions of earth directly under the brush canopy. Stripping off his shirt, he wrapped it, bandana-like, over his mouth and nose, then wriggled into the pit he'd created and began scooping dirt back over himself. Once his head was covered, Sydney settled down, leaving his eyes and nose some space beneath the shirt. Soil, sand and pebbles irritated his ears, while tiny branches poked unpleasantly, but Sydney settled in, breathing calmly. *No different than hiding from those bloody blacks in my country–or in the pestholes where I was a mercenary, picking the bastards off like ducks in a gallery. They never caught on to a proper ambush. Not hard now, either. Be patient. Just be patient. Dying for a cigarette, though. Of course, how would I do it under here?*

He could hear the copters hovering to and fro for two hours. They'd work in circles, hitting Sydney's hiding place at twenty-minute intervals. Then their noise grew dim and, finally, everything went quiet. Eventually, the chorus of disrupted insects kicked up. Fast little crawlies commenced their rounds as Sydney wriggled free of his earthen shroud.

He spent a long while clearing the soil and alkaline material from his hair, where it all had stuck to his perspiration-drenched skin, under his undershorts and along his legs. Irritation needled his vulnerable flesh. *Damn lucky you didn't get visited by scorpions or the like,* he told himself. *This will all wash out.*

The sun was deep in the west, leaving the landscape pinkish and much cooler. The few clouds were pastel purple, tinged with the last pink of the day.

Shaking soil and sand from the mask he had fashioned from his shirt, Sydney pulled it over his head. Far to the left, lights twinkled on in the Grasslands. Dinner time was approaching and residents would be incredulously watching the recent fiasco so close to their cozy world. *Well, it's time for me to meet my fans, so to speak.*

He strode with determination toward the unsuspecting subdivision. Not once did his disciplined mind go back to Dalia or the setbacks he had encountered. To a professional like Sidney, that was water under the damn. It was all about now.

***

Guerrero, Stone and Flynn sat up late in Flynn's office. "Guess we call this a 'debriefing'," Guerrero said. "Lot of our guys are already heading home." The coffee cup he drank from read "Law & Order SUV" and showed a photo of its leading actress, Mariska Hargitay.

Flynn munched a stale donut that he had requisitioned from the cleaning crew. "Guess you right. Our boys from outta town, also. Ain't much more tuh do, ah'd say." He looked at Stedmier, whose expression was far away. "Why you so quiet, Sted? Ain't yuh happy we stopped it? Shore, the medical folks said we gonna have some virus cases, but, hell, not nearly what it could'a been."

The young captain roused himself. He scratched under his eye, his lips pressing tight. "Cain't say. Theh's jus' something not right—yuh know, like an itch way below where yuh cain't reach. This guy . . . so cool. So prepared he had a damn grenade launcha'. An' we jus' assume he's daid? Ah jus' don' know. Wish one a' those people at the concert coulda given our artists a decent description, but not a one could . . . all too busy whoopin' it up. 'Tall'— mebbe, cause he was kneeling tuh git the hat; an' blondish hair—mebbe. Sheet, if this fellah was across the road shootin' us the fingah, we wouldn' even recognize him. Sheet!" He slammed the desk with a solid *thud.*

"We had coptahs all ovah the place, Sted." Flynn thrust the remainder of his donut in Steadmier's direction. "He ain't no lizard, damn it. I say he's fried all ovah thet car a his, like a sunny side up egg . . . tha's what ah think. Stop frettin' yoreself."

Guerrero and Stone nodded mutually and rose. "Well, we're pretty satisfied and so are our bosses, gentlemen. So we'll be leaving," Guerrero said. "Got a bit of a drive."

Stone leaned his long frame over the desk. "Thanks, both of you. A pleasure working together," he winked, "although we can't admit it to Washington."

The rangers laughed and waved back as both men headed out. "Catch yuh next time," Flynn yelled, although neither he nor Stedmier were sure the departing pair had heard. Either way, there was no response.

Flynn sorted out his desk as he prepared to leave. "You jus' ain't happy ah yuh, Sted. Mebbe aftuh a good night's sleep . . . Lord knows we need it."

Stedmier's smile was a tired one. "Yeah, mebbe. I'll be headin' back fu'st thing. S'long, Toby."

"Catch yuh next time, Sted. Gonna call the wife afore ah go. Give the ol' laduh a chance tuh git her lovah packin', 'cause ahm comin' home regular agin."

Laughing, Stedmier left the room.

***

The traffic on 158 was thinning and Sydney had no trouble crossing over, unnoticed. He walked along the wall to an unmanned entry, adopting the relaxed pace of someone walking off his dinner. Residents, engaged in a similar pursuit, exchanged friendly greetings.

As evening light grew dimmer, Sydney became far more attentive to his surroundings. *I need a car, but it can't be reported for at least a few days. That means someone alone or out of town. And how would I know who's out of town? So . . .*

***

The Estates was a typical friendly Texas community. Lights were on and curtains or blinds were undrawn. Sydney steered clear of neighborhood dogs, many of whom barked incessantly in the hazy twilight. One by one, lights clicked off although TV screens still blazed in many of the sizeable brick and stone homes. Each had double garages and vaulted roofs—indicative of high ceilings. All had pools and nice sized lots.

Sydney was especially interested in the cul-de-sacs backing onto open land. Activity would be less noticeable around isolated houses. He avoided those with indications of children: either spilled toys on their yards, or noisy voices inside. Eventually, he came upon a conservative Ford. It was ten or better years of age as opposed to the new models populating the affluent community. The car sat outside of an open garage whose inside was cluttered with tools, furniture, and boxes of all sizes. *Hoarders. Good. That's what old people with memories and grown children do.*

Aside from *humming* insects, nothing moved in the heavy, darkening air. Glancing around, the tall man assured himself that not a soul was nearby and, because of its isolated position, no neighboring house had a clear view of the home. Sydney quietly skirted flowering hedges sprinkled by light from what he suspected was a kitchen window. Sure enough, there were leftover dishes in the sink. But he was especially attracted by the single place setting on a table with vestiges of a meal.

Suddenly, a man of about seventy or more entered, not fit but not doddering, with thin white hair but decisive movements. He started clearing. Sydney ducked to the side as the laden man headed for the sink. After a few minutes, the kitchen light extinguished and, farther down, another snapped on. Sydney edged toward it and saw a bedroom with twin beds. One had a crumpled spread, splayed upper sheet and a pillow hanging precariously off the side. The other was pristine. For a moment, the room's occupant looked sadly at the made-up twin. Next to it was a wedding picture on a table with clock radio. Then the elderly man stepped into his closet, removing a standard size suitcase of shiny, unbreakable material. This he hefted onto his own bed and commenced packing.

As a consummate judge of human actions—which he had to be—Sydney surmised from the man's melancholic deference toward the second bed that the gentlemen's wife had recently died. Also, that he was going away. *To visit his children or an escape. Either way this will suit me perfectly.* Sydney stuck to the shadows as long as possible, then darted to the Ford. Its trunk was open in anticipation of luggage. *Too easy,* Sydney smiled. *I must be living right.* The expression's irony was not lost on him as he silently slid into the back seat.

A tuneless whistling caused him to duck down behind the passenger side. Light from a quarter moon left him plenty of shadow. As he hunched, waiting, Sydney contemplated. *I could take him now, no problem, but it would be better if he drives out, so any neighbors can see him leaving.* Sydney bent over and stretched, aware that his knees ached, slightly. *Lot of walking today,* he rationalized. *He'll be getting in soon.*

Sure enough, after one brief trip back to the house, the old man *slammed* his front door and, still whistling, closed the trunk. Then the driver's door *thunked* shut. Next he adjusted his radio. Willie Nelson's "Always On My Mind" blanketed Sydney's gentle shift to avoid cramping. The tune suddenly seemed profoundly sad. He didn't allow himself to question why.

CHAPTER 26 ALWAYS CHECK THE TRUNK

The British Airways agent behind the desk at Dallas/Fort Worth International was quite taken by the tall man who spoke the King's English, but with an odd accent. *South African* she guessed, rightly.

Once he pocketed his ticket to London, he smiled, inquiring where he could smoke before the flight. She pointed the way and felt a twinge of homesickness as he turned and pulled out a box of John Player Special Blues. When she stared, he remarked, "Can't find my own brand here," and walked off. He never inquired as to her taking notice of the foreign cigarettes. Nor did he ever learn that they were her father's favorite back in London.

***

Two days after Stedmier and he parted company, Flynn was on the phone to him in Austin. "Don' think this means anythaing . . . but ah know you got a porcupine up yuh ass 'bout thet terrorist fellah. "

"What?" Stedmier said without laughing at Flynn's typically inane characterization. "What?" he asked, louder this time.

"Well, some lady in Odessa called into local po-lice yesta'day. Seems her daddy didn't show up drivin' ovah from Midland. Las' night, our all-points found his cah at DFW with daddy in th' trunk. Only reason ah mention it is the old guy lived in thet community right across from where our boys went down in thet copter the otha' day.

Don' mean—"

"*Yes it does!*" yelled Stedmier. "*Yes it fuckin' does!*"

The young ranger who heard the phone *crash* against the floor rushed into Stedmier's office.

His tanned captain brushed by. " I'm out fuh the day, Collins. An' less'n the pres'dent is shot, ah don' wanna hear nothin' from nobody."

Collins stared at the cell phone lying against the bottom of the wall. He picked it up. The cracked screen was utterly blank. *Now, how could I call him even if the president was shot?* he wondered. Shaking his head, he placed the shattered instrument back upon Stedmier's desk.

EPILOGUE IT'S FAR FROM OVER

Senator Arlo Grossman's aide looked uncomfortable, even when facing Kelly Frank's shapely knees. "It's only been a few days since the Senator's passing and with the outbreak here in Texas, well . . . excuse the office."

Kelly's voice was low, sympathetic as she smiled at heavyset Warren Jacobs. His unkempt brownish hair and stubble were not in keeping with his position as a senator's aide. Boxes and files strewn around the small office confirmed his imminent departure from the Senate Office Building. "The virus has us all worried, Warren, even in Washington, but thank goodness it seems to have been caught early and highly limited, thanks to the Rangers and F.B.I."

The young man regained some positivity. "Yes. Attendees at the music festival were contact traced and quarantined. Those returning to Mexico and other parts will be a problem, what with its extremely contagious nature." He puffed out his ample cheeks. "But it could have been a lot worse."

"Sure, Warren, much worse." Kelly pursed her pouty lips. "But it will stop the fracking for a while . . . Warren, the Senator was opposed to fracking, wasn't he?"

"Sure, we all were." His fleshy cheeks reddened. "It destroys our planet." His eyes narrowed. "Why, aren't you?"

"Sure, who isn't," she said with a vigorous nod. "Warren, you know, that information the Rangers found—"

His voice rose the next instant and he looked very young and very helpless. "The Senator had *nothing t*o do with that and smearing his name—"

Kelly's long fingers spread. "No, no. I know that. We may never know how they showed up in Midland in that car. It could have been hundreds of people. But you know there has been a lot of talk. The Senator was a bitter enemy of oil . . . and since I've met Mimi," she waited for her proffered intimacy with the widow to register, "I want to spare her further pain by excluding her dear husband's memory from ugly speculation. With a few facts, I can help her and her family."

At the mention of Gross's wife, water filled the young man's eyes. "Yes, yes," he sniveled. "Mimi deserves that. What can I tell you?"

"Well," Kelley paused to reflect for his benefit, although she knew exactly what she wanted. "If I knew who he might have met with . . . just before . . . that could help establish his frame of mind. You know, family concerns, health, things that had nothing to do with Midland."

The young man consulted his computer. "Yes, of course. Anything to shift the focus from this slanderous idea that the Senator, God rest his soul, could be involved."

"Exactly," the reporter encouraged.

"Well, his schedule was pretty clear for the week before . . . only a Mr. Hans Gerlinger of the Swiss Embassy—I don't have his title—and he were out for lunch a few afternoons before. But that's not unusual. They were friends." Jacobs shook his heavy head and shrugged.

"That's about it."

Kelley rose slowly, allowing Jacobs one final peek. "Thank you so much, Warren, and don't forget to send Mimi my regards. I know you're busy packing, so I'll show myself out."

***

His mustache makes him look like a refined Hitler. Kelley sat in the four-story Swiss Embassy. *Rich country, rich embassy,* she noted. His office had velvet drapes and glistening walnut furniture, indicating stature, but the man was evasive about his official capacity when asked. "I am a 'Jack of all Trades' but not a master of none," he said as he smiled through perfectly even— if just a little horsey— teeth.

After offering her a perfectly foamed latte from the expensive machine near his desk, Gerlinger said, "My meetings are generally kept private. I have to maintain my neutrality with the representatives of many nations, you understand."

Kelly doubted that her legs would be of any benefit to this interview, so she kept them primly crossed. "I certainly understand. I'm only doing this to ease the widow's pain because there are rumors—"

"Ah, yes. Washington and its rumors," he said, nodding his head.

Whether he actually accepted her excuse, or merely enjoyed evading, Kelley wasn't sure, but with a whimsical twist of his lips, Gerlinger decided. "Well, I did introduce him to Uri Spanov of the Russian Embassy here. His official title is questionable, but they all are, you know."

Kelly's breath quickened. "Thank you. You say I'll find him at the Embassy?" At once, Kelly understood the man's willingness to jeopardize his "neutrality." With disappointment, she heard him reply, "Oh, no, not anymore. My friend, Spanov, was suddenly called away back to Russia. You know what the means. We might not be seeing him anymore." His taunting eyes were alert for her reaction. When she didn't accommodate, the suave man forced a smile. "More coffee, my dear young lady?"

The young reporter knew she would not forget the satiric glow in Gerlinger's pale eyes as she declined and abruptly left.

***

A day later, Kelly sat before a young man, with well-tailored, youthfully designed clothes, at the Ministry of Foreign Affairs of the Russian Federation, inside its hulking, ultra-modern D.C. embassy. He came across as remarkably handsome in a broad-faced Slavic way. His brown eyes never left her face to peruse Kelly's knees or thighs. *Can't win 'em all*, she thought.

The young man looked puzzled. "And what is your interest in Mr. Spanov?"

"Well, he was referred to me for a story on the assimilation of those employed here to our American way of life. He is a cultural attaché, isn't he?"

In a moment of confusion, the young man's composure slipped. Then his smile returned. "Yes, yes, of course—there are so many here and I am new—"

Kelly smiled. *More used to them with their military titles, aren't you, but you never call them that to outsiders.*

"Sure, I know how it is . . . uh?"

"Ivan, just call me Ivan, Miss?"

"Just Kelly will do."

"Yes, Kelly." He bowed behind the desk. "Well, I regret to say Mr. Spanov is not here at present…but," his smile was dazzling, "we have a number of attachés who would be pleased to answer your questions."

Kelly made sure to pose her mouth in the extra pretty pout before letting off an exaggerated sigh. "He was so highly recommended, though. Perhaps I can arrange an appointment another day?"

For the first time, the poised young man looked uncomfortable. "You see, I will have to check . . . I'm new and not aware of all the schedules . . ." He reached for a phone. "You will excuse me." After nodding several times, Ivan lowered the phone. "I want you to have th-the best help, so I will take you to someone who is better suited." He rose from his chair.

As an excellent observer, Kelly noted concern on his unblemished face.

"Please follow me." The tone was now formal, his speech stilted.

No more chance of a date for me, thought Kelly.

A sinewy man with large hands stood in the doorway of a large office far down the hall. "Thank you, Ivan," he said as he dismissed Kelly's escort. Ivan left without a goodbye.

"I am the Assistant Ambassador." His handshake was powerful. Kelly grimaced but he appeared not to notice. "My name is Roshenko."

No first name, thought Kelly. *The level of cordiality has declined dramatically.* "Thank you for seeing me." Her smile had no impact on the man.

"You are doing an article on assimilation of our staff to America? That is correct?"

"Yes."

"Then why wouldn't any other cultural attaché do for your purposes?" Roshenko made no attempt at charm. His cold eyes were skeptical.

"He was recommended—"

"Well, my dear young lady, Spanov is on assignment elsewhere and he may not be available for a long time—"

"I can wait..."

His drooping lids made slits of his eyes. "A *very* long time. These things happen in a big organization such as ours." Deliberately consulting his heavy, expensive watch, he said, "Now, can I introduce you to another very competent member of our staff. I assure you he is very knowledgeable about your topic. Or," his eyes narrowed even further, "won't that be sufficient?"

"That would be fine . . . Oh, I didn't realize the time," said the young reporter, glimpsing at her watch, "and . . . " she shrugged apologetically, "I have a deadline. Where does the time go?"

"Yes," said Roshenko, "where indeed?"

"Yes," said Kelley. "I will reschedule."

"Of course," the man agreed. "At your convenience." His cold eyes mocked her. "I will ring for Ivan to see you out."

"Thank you." Kelly responded in a tone that, for her, was unnaturally subdued.

***

A jagged sheet of sunlight slid across Fred Goldfarb's desk from the nearby slanted blind. It then made its way across Kelly's lovely knees and, though he fought it for all he was worth, the editor succumbed, as usual. What he heard killed his voyeurism. Cold. "Kelly, stop . . . just *stop!*"

Her eyes were feverish with excitement. "Why? This is *huge!* Grossman was part of that plague down in Texas. And he was working with the Russians! Why else has Spanov just disappeared right after? I said they met and . . ." she jabbed a purple nail at her copy sheet, "confirmed by the Swiss guy—*they did!* You taught me to always get confirmation, *I did*—"

"Fat chance he'll ever re-confirm this." The heavy editor's bald head was awash in perspiration as he flung a finger toward the paper in her hand. "Do you think he's crazy . . . *like you?*"

She was out of her chair. "Why? *The fucking plans came from the Senate!* They say so right on them. And the Rangers—"

Now Fred was up, too. "The Rangers have been told to keep quiet after that initial interview with a local crime reporter, and now they're not saying a word."

"Nearly two thousand killed so far and many more in quarantine. Shit, Fred, this could be deadlier than the last Covid . . . or Wuhan, take your choice. If they hadn't stopped those two when they did—"

"A disaster. I agree, Kelly." The old editor tried to breathe slowly, willing his pulse to stop pounding through his veins. "As it is, fracking will be set back a year. And the politicians, now that they've recovered from their shock about the new President's energy leanings, will tie it up a whole lot longer. But, that does not prove that a dead senator conspired with the Russians . . . or that he even had anything to do with those plans. Or that this Russian, Spanov, did."

"Why can't we interview Spanov?"

"The Russians have said that is completely impossible. There are even rumors of a serious accident at his dacha—"

"Oh, sure. *Fuck, Fred. A damn cover-up and we—*"

"And we haven't got a way to do anything but..." Goldfarb smiled, tilting his head toward the outraged girl "...speculate." Then he took her hands in his. "And speculation kills a paper." He shrugged, opening his palms upward. "At least when you're small like us and don't have the big money like the *Times* or the *Post* behind you." Sighing, he settled back into his chair. "Please sit."

After she did, Goldfarb said slowly and somewhat harshly to his favorite young reporter. "We will not take this any further. You know who runs the publishing world and how *they* feel. Big energy is out and Texans will be lucky if they even have working oil wells in a few years . . . and, Kelly, let the Senator stay dead and his family have peace because . . . *we can't do a fucking thing about it.* So drop it . . . *or I swear I'll drop you! The end!"*

All at once, Kelly understood the rage and frustration prompting his uncharacteristic outburst. The enthusiasm of the past few days vanished like smoke in a strong breeze and her feeling of futility mirrored that of her frustrated mentor. "Sure, boss," she answered quietly.

***

Three months later, the man sometimes known as Phillip Sydney and sometimes by other names, sipped a cognac from the balcony of his villa overlooking the Yacht Club of Monte Carlo. Traffic entering the Tunnel du Larvotto appeared sporadically between gaps in the stand of island pines directly below.

The Mediterranean breeze, although unnecessary to mitigate the moderate temperatures of Monaco, brought the sweet, fruity fragrance of the Princess Charlene roses which proliferated along the surrounding hillsides.

Although well rested and considerably wealthier from his recent endeavor, Sydney's anger was as real as the day that he had determined that one or more of his employers had betrayed him. A vein in his temple throbbed as the catastrophic ending of his recent mission intruded upon the serenity of the peaceful setting. It was by no means the first time. *They sold me out completely, forced me to kill someone I cared about. That wasn't my plan. My plan would have worked! And the excess killing. The brave men in the helicopter . . . the old man. A waste.*

Sydney studied the light permeating his cognac in an attempt to assuage his burgeoning rage. But, even with his superlative mental control, it was not to be denied. *I cannot allow this betrayal to go unpunished. Otherwise, others could sell me out if the going got too rough for them. And that would make me expendable—which I certainly am not!*

Inadvertently, he had crushed the delicate Oakmont snifter's stem. Gaping at the sun-brightened remnants strewn upon the mosaic floor only augmented Sydney's rage. "They'll learn," he vowed. "Oh, yes. Whoever they were, *I will* make them an example!"

The blue ice in Phillip Sydney's eyes glowed. *"Anyone hiring me will rather die than betray me again!"* he vowed.

Staring at the trickle of blood spreading along the hand clutching the remnants of his broken snifter, he wrapped it with a cocktail napkin from a stack on a nearby table. The napkin's front was covered with a circle of red, blue and green sombreros — a much larger orange one with yellow tassels occupied the center. He lit a cigarette and watched the thin strand of smoke swirl in the gentle breeze. Sydney's lips twisted into a wry smile. *The only things that I'll let do me in, someday, will be these damn cigarettes.*

ABOUT THE AUTHOR

After attending Cornell University and University of Pennsylvania School of Law, the author became an Assistant Attorney General of New York State and subsequently a Region Counsel for General Electric Company. Since that time, he has developed real estate projects in a number of states, and for the past thirty years his Florida firm has managed investments for clients in fourteen states. As an avid skier, he has attempted almost every slope in the U.S. and some in Europe. Currently he practices self-defense, works out, bike rides and swims. He has performed in plays both in California and Florida, including *6 Rms Riv Vu* and *Sound of Music*. He began writing in 1992 as a hobby; which has now become a passion. Burt lives in Florida with his wife, Mary, and a terribly spoiled cat named Furgie.

www.ingramcontent.com/pod-product-compliance
Lightning Source LLC
Chambersburg PA
CBHW052110030426
42335CB00025B/2919